1-16-76

New Woman
New Earth

In this book, acclaimed author Rosemary Radford Ruether studies the relationships between sexism, racism and capitalism and how these ideologies and structures have developed our ideas on women. But in this unusual study, she also probes the ideological images of women as created through religion, particularly in the Judeo-Christian tradition. This volume discusses separately, then combines, all these concepts to lead ultimately to an analysis of the formation of our images of contemporary women.

Professor Ruether first probes the images of women in religion, which are still sanctioned by the traditional churches, and religion's modern substitutes, particularly psychology. She relates these images to the socio-economic status of women today.

She then studies the relationship between the inferiorization of women and the negative images projected onto despised minorities such as Jews and Blacks. This interstructuring of sexism is also discussed in relation to other forms of social prejudice, making apparent

(continued on back flap)

(continued from front flap)

that racism and sexism are not just "parallel" but are part of a larger social phenomenon in our history. Sexism is also intimately wedded to the biblically derived "domination of nature motif" both ideologically and in the structuring of home and work.

The relationship of these many themes finally points in the same direction: toward the integration and radical transformation of these negative images and social realities in an egalitarian, communitarion, ecologically balanced world.

Rosemary Radford Ruether

SEXIST IDEOLOGIES
AND HUMAN LIBERATION

A Crossroad Book
THE SEABURY PRESS · NEW YORK

The Seabury Press
815 Second Avenue
New York, N.Y. 10017

Library of Congress Cataloging in Publication Data

Ruether, Rosemary Radford.
    New woman/new earth.

    "A Crossroad book."
    Bibliography: p.
    Includes index.
    1. Sex discrimination against women—Addresses, essays, lectures. 2. Women in Christianity—Addresses, essays, lectures. 3. Race discrimination—Addresses, essays, lectures. 4. Sex role—Addresses, essays, lectures. I. Title.
HQ1154.R83   261.8'34'1   75-17649
ISBN 0-8164-1205-7

Printed in the United States of America

These essays are dedicated to my children
   Rebecca, David, and Mimi,
Who inherit the world we have made,
   Who must start to build a
   New Earth

Set up waymarks for yourself,
   make yourself guideposts;
consider well the highway,
   the road by which you went.
Return, O virgin Israel,
   return to these your cities.
How long will you waver,
   O wandering daughter?
For the Lord has created a new
   thing on the earth:
   the female overcomes the warrior.
                     Jeremiah 31:21–22

Contents

Acknowledgments   ix
Preface   xi

PART ONE · Religion and Sexism: The Unholy Alliance   1
1 · The Descent of Woman: Symbol and Social Condition   3
2 · Mistress of Heaven: The Meaning of Mariology   36
3 · Guarding the Sanctuary: Sexism and Ministry   63
PART TWO · Strange Bedfellows: Women and Other Aliens   87
4 · Witches and Jews: The Demonic Alien in Christian Culture   89
5 · Between the Sons of White and the Sons of Blackness: Racism and Sexism in America   115
PART THREE · Women: The Last Revolution   131
6 · The Psychoanalytic Revolution: Friend or Enemy of Women?   137
7 · The First and Final Proletariat: Socialism and Feminism   162
8 · New Woman and New Earth: Women, Ecology, and Social Revolution   186

Select Bibliography: Women's History   215
Index   219

Acknowledgments

THESE CHAPTERS WERE DEVELOPED WITH THE HELP OF VARIOUS lectureships where the material of this book was explored. Some of the material on psychoanalysis and on socialism was given in lectures at Wheaton College, Norton, Massachusetts, in February 1974. The material on witches and Jews, on racism and sexism, and on ecology was delivered in the Homer Armstrong Lectures at Kalamazoo College in October 1974. Some of the material on pre-Christian religious images of women, on Mariology and on sexism and ministry made up the Kellogg Lectures at Episcopal Divinity School, Cambridge, Massachusetts, February 1975. Earlier drafts of this material on Mariology and ecclesiology were also explored in the Vosburgh Lectures at Drew Theological School in May 1973.

Preface

THIS BOOK IS MADE UP OF A GROUP OF SKETCHES ON THE basic issue of sexism. These chapters cover overlapping ground, but from different perspectives. They study the ideologies, religious and secular, which have supported sexism. They also look at the interrelation of sexism with other structures of oppression, such as race, class, and technological power, which have built Western civilization on the basis of domination and alienation. The totality of these structures, today, is tending toward the denouement of the entire human project.

It does not seem to me possible to draw a counterplan for an alternative world and human self-understanding in comparable detail or assurance. At this point in history one can do little more than try to recognize the crisis points of contradiction in the present system and, at that horizon, try to imagine what an alternative might look like. Moreover, I do not find in women's history an existing alternative, either in a prepatriarchal period of history or hidden within patriarchal history. Threads of both alternatives can be traced. But these are broken histories, overshadowed by the great historic reality of women shaped into "Eve," the female created by the male. These broken fragments begin to swell into a real alternative, not just for women, but for humanity and the earth, only now. Only today have large numbers of people begun to suspect that patriarchy, which has shaped human history until now, is unviable for future development and indeed is fast proving unable to maintain the survival of humankind on the planet. This is the period when the women's movement, properly understood, encompasses all other liberation movements.

These chapters cover a great deal of ground. They try to capture the lineaments of a crisis of human society in our own day, but one which is rooted in thousands of years of history. I do not apologize for a certain generality. Women's studies is addressing itself to a different task from that which has shaped traditional academic scholarship. For this reason its criteria of competence must also be different. First of all this is because the women's movement must encompass a far larger history than other movements. Liberation movements begin at the point of the subjugation of their people. Black Americans begin their story with the slave ships of European colonialism in the sixteenth century. Latin Americans begin their story in the same period. But the subjugation of women begins in prehistoric culture. The woman's story must encompass the entire scope of the human dilemma. Moreover the issue of sexism crosses and includes every field of specialization. Women cannot confine themselves to short sections of time or separations of fields, which give established scholarship its illusion of total mastery of its subject. To be sure, very specific studies, limited in time and field, are needed. But even these studies must presuppose this comprehensive setting of the issue.

Women's studies do not pretend to an ethical neutrality. This stance is actually a ruling class ideology. Neutrality hides a commitment to the status quo. All liberation scholarship is advocacy scholarship. This should not make it any less objective in analyzing what has actually been the case. Liberation movements have no stake in a mythological history which falsifies the past. But this objectivity is in the service of passionate commitment. We search history anxiously, trying to understand the sources of its massive failure. We look for signs of hope that a new beginning is possible. The commitment of women today continues to be what it has always been: a commitment to the survival of children and of the earth. But today this commitment to the future of life also must make women the implacable foes of those systems of ruling-class male power which have dominated human history and self-understanding.

The issue of language has become very important for feminists in exposing the sexist bias of the dominant consciousness. Teaching at a black institution since 1966, I have been a latecomer to the language issue. Lacking women students, this issue was not being raised by those around me. Blacks were busy making their own analysis of racist ideology and its reflection in culture. Language is the prime reflection of the power of the ruling group to define reality in its own terms and demote oppressed groups into invisibility. Women, more than any other group, are overwhelmed by a linguistic form that excludes them from visible existence.

However, I have some caveats about the prescribed methods for solving the problem of sexist language. As long as the system of male domination prevails, linguistic modifications can be fed back into this system, creating the appearance of change that becomes more difficult to criticize. To carefully change the generic *man* to the generic *human* makes little sense if the word *human* also is described as *he*. It is also delusory to speak of present or past roles of public life as "he and she," when she was not included. Such a procedure can promote a false consciousness which covers the actual history of discrimination by pretending that "she" was actually an equal participant in that reality defined by male ideologists as "humanity." I have followed a different procedure in these writings. When speaking of situations which were male dominated, I have used *he* and even *men,* but have indicated what this word really meant, i.e., ruling-class males. Only when I speak of ideals, when I speak of liberation and the hope for a new society of equal participation have I used words such as *human-kind* which are intended to point beyond not just sexism, but race and class domination as well.

These chapters attempt to lay a groundwork for recognizing the interrelation of ideology and social structure in the history of sexism. They span both the traditional form of ideology, religion, and its modern scientific heirs, such as psychology. They try to show that all these ideologies are the cultural superstructure for a system of male domination which is socioeconomic and systemic in character. These ideologies try to make that social structure look "natural," inevitable and divinely given. To change consciousness is only a beginning. For culture and consciousness themselves are merely the ratifiers of a social system which demands the relegating of women to auxiliary and menial positions. The transformation of consciousness is the servant of a struggle to transform this entire social system in its human and ecological relationships. I hope these various essays will add up to an experience for the reader that makes these interrelationships recognizable. Such essays are not the last word. Much detailed work by specialists in many areas is needed. But one hopes that they can be one of the initial words which, at least, names these various components and tries to locate them in their connection with each other. If these chapters have done that much, they will have accomplished their task.

PART ONE

Religion and Sexism: The Unholy Alliance

The Descent of Woman:
Symbol and Social Condition

ENGELS, IN HIS CLASSIC STUDY *The Origin and History of the Family*, defined the subjugation of women as the first oppressor-oppressed relation, the foundation of all other class and property relations.[1] But in modern liberation movements, the "Woman Question" is often the last question to be raised, the question most resisted by those with otherwise "liberal" views on social questions, the issue most readily discarded after the revolution. This is the one area where a doctrine of "fixed natures," dictating a fixed social destiny, is still accepted in the very circles which would reject such stereotypes applied to poor people or other races. Anthropological theories, which once gave scientific respectability to racism, are no longer acceptable in academia (although they seem to be enjoying a comeback). But the psychoanalytical pseudo science that reinstated the traditional doctrines of female inferiority are still preached in those same academic circles.

The reason why sexism is the "last cause" is doubtless because its stereotypes are older and deeper in our culture than any others. It also affects the identity and personal support system of such (male) liberals more than any other issue. Sexual symbolism is foundational to the perception of order and relationship that has been built up in cultures. The psychic organization of consciousness, the dualistic view of the self and the world, the hierarchical concept of society, the relation of humanity and nature, and of God and creation—all these relationships have been modeled on sexual dualism. Therefore the liberation of women attacks the basic stereotypes of authority, identity, and the structural relations of "reality."

The male ideology of the "feminine" that we have inherited in the West seems to be rooted in a self-alienated experience of the body and the world, projecting upon the sexual other the lower half of these dualisms. As Simone de Beauvoir pointed out many years ago in her classic study, *The Second Sex*, in male-dominated societies, it is always woman who is the "other," the antithesis over against which one defines "authentic" (male) selfhood. But a repressive view of the alien female was also the model for the inferiorization of other subjugated groups, lower classes, and conquered races. Subjugated groups are perceived through similar stereotypes, not because they are alike, but because the same dominant group (ruling-class males) are doing the perceiving. All oppressed peoples tend then to be seen as lacking in rationality, volition, and capacity for autonomy. The characteristics of repressed bodiliness are attributed to them: passivity, sensuality, irrationality, and dependency. The dominant race, class, and sexual caste, on the other hand, model their self-image after ego or consciousness. They are the true humanity or selfhood, possessing intrinsically the qualities of initiative, reason, capacity for autonomy and higher virtues. These myths are still with us. Only a few years ago the Episcopal bishop of California denied the capacity of women for ordination on the grounds that only males possess the capacity for "initiative" that represents the "potency" of God.[2] To examine the stereotypes of the feminine, therefore, is to open up the basic points of social tension and their ideological rationalization.

More than other liberation movements women are still plagued with the aetiological question: how did it all begin? Behind this question is the supposition that anything so ancient must be "natural" and therefore "just." Women are thrown into the defensive posture of trying to prove that they have the capacity for full humanity because "once upon a time. . . ." The myth of an unfallen Eden is a symbolic point of reference for liberation thought of all kinds, leading Marxists to posit a primordial "primitive communism," and blacks to lift up images of brilliant ancient black kingdoms. For women, the myth of "primitive matriarchy" has been their Eden, the proof that they had capacities which were repressed by the later development of unjust power that concealed these capacities and prevented them from appearing. The full-blown lineaments of this concept of matriarchy, as developed by nineteenth-century thinkers such as Bachofen and taken up more recently in writings such as Elizabeth Gould Davis's *The First Sex*, seem to me unhistorical.[3] Nevertheless I do believe that we can begin to sketch out today the lines of the real historical development whereby the female person, possessing a different but strong body and an equal capacity for thought and culture, was subverted and made to appear physiologically and intellectually inferior. Unfortunately, anthropology, like other social sciences, has been pervasively sexist, and therefore much of the more detailed work on the links between tribal and urban cultures in the history of women is still to be developed. Yet the basic lines of development can be drawn in a way that may reveal no primitive female-dominated Eden, but nevertheless will prove more useful to understanding the real history than have bad anthropology and faulty history. The stages of this history are also reflected in the changing ideology or symbolization of the "feminine" in (male-defined) culture. I will try to sketch the broad lines of this development of social reality and its symbolic rationalization through three stages, each stage assimilating and building upon the earlier one, even as it hides it from view. These stages I have called (1) the Conquest of the Mother, (2) the Negation of the Mother, and (3) the Sublimation of the Mother.

THE CONQUEST OF THE MOTHER

The myth of primitive matriarchy was compounded from two culturally disparate sources: (a) matrilineal and matrilocal culture among primitives, and evidence that a similar stage of society existed behind the classical societies of antiquity, and (b) the predominance of mother-goddess figures in the nonbiblical religions of Mediterranean and Near Eastern peoples. The problem with this fusion of anthropology and classical studies is that the first type of data refers to neolithic peoples, while the second comes from developed urbanized cultures up through the first centuries of the Christian era. These were cultures which were patriarchal and often oppressively so, such as the fifth-century Greeks. The two types of data cannot be conflated but must be distinguished. Then we may be able to find the relationship between an early tribal culture (where social complementarity of male and female roles was more equalitarian) and the development of symbolic systems in which the strong role of women (which still persists in agrarian and handicraft economy, together with the centrality of the mother experienced in the first stage of every child's life) projected a world-view which imaged the mother as the primordial source of life. But this symbolic view of the woman as "Mother Nature" does not promote female social equality, but represents the fundamental stage of the cooptation of the female into a power system seen from a male point of view. The female is seen as a life force, to be used or worshiped in relation to a male-centered definition of humanity, rather than as a person from her own point of view.

Generally, village culture was more equalitarian, in terms of sex and class relations, than the city society that began with the urban revolution. Yet in the early hunting and agricultural stages, biological differences between men and women created a complementarity of work roles. Men were the hunters and warriors. From this they generally took exclusive control of the political arena. Those religious rites which sanctify political power became male. Women's power centered in economic life. As food gatherers and perhaps the discoverers of gardening, women often commanded the transformatory processes that turned the raw into the cooked, herbs into medicines, raw materials into clothes, baskets, and pots. In short, women had their role and bargaining power in the initial forms of agriculture, economic processing, manufacture, medicine, and marketing. This economic role did not disappear with the urban revolution. It continued in peasant life. Even great latifundia were often ruled by women as extensions of family economy, while the males occupied themselves with war and politics. As long as the economy was centered in the family, woman had social bargaining power, despite the development of patriarchal political systems that defined her as dependent and rightless.

Two critical turning points are important for the analysis of the socioeconomic history of women. The first is the transition from tribal or village to urban life. The urban revolution originally affected only a small segment of society, with most society remaining in agrarian and family-centered handicraft economies. But it created a new elite group of males whose power was no longer based on the physical prowess of the hunter or warrior, but on the inherited monopoly of political power and knowledge. Females were equally capable of entering into this kind of power on equal terms, but instead they were excluded from it and consigned to an ornamental role—with occasional exceptions. The cultural spokesmen for ruling-class males began to develop ideologies of both class and female inferiority to justify their position. These ideologies trickled down to the lower classes, shaping earlier patriarchal systems into a more strictly servile view of women's work. Since these ideologies of female psychic inferiority contradict women's experience of themselves, they must constantly be reinforced by artificial repression of female development and misogynist attacks on women designed to intimidate any nascent criticism and to bolster male egoism. The constant drip of vicious antifemaleness, which characterizes all classical cultures from the ancient Greek poets and Hebrew scribes to the psychoanalytic high priests and pundits of our own times, reveals the ever unsatisfactorily completed task of shaping women into the compliant, auxiliary being which she is supposed to be, according to male ideology, and repressing, in each generation of women, the dawning experience of larger capacities.

The second important period for women's history is the development of mass industrialization, which diffuses urbanization over more and more of the world and shifts economic production increasingly from the family to a work place separated from the home. For the first time women as a group became marginal to production and economically dependent on male work for survival. Even though many poor women went out to work in the factory at this time, they were still tied, as women, to providing the procreative and domestic support systems of male work. Working women, therefore, became fundamentally handicapped as competitors with males in the work sphere.

But this new depletion of women's economic role in the home through industrialization also created a new restlessness in middle- and upper-class women who were left with insufficient meaningful work in the home. A feminist movement, which was expressed in only a few isolated voices in past centuries, began to become a mass movement in the nineteenth century. Women began to rebel against the traditional ideologies of subjugation and to demand civil rights and entrance into education and professions. Working-class women in the factories were swept into the union movement, but found themselves opposed not only by the owning classes, but by male unionists as well. Industrialization completed the earlier marginalization of women's place culturally and politically by economic marginalization. But it also created a new level of contradiction between women's experience of their own capacities and the shrunken and dependent place assigned to them—and so led to the rise of a mass feminist struggle to alter the classical images and roles of women.

Feminism should not idealize the tribal period as a "golden age" for women's autonomy and power. The complementary work roles found in that period may have been more equalitarian than in subsequent stages, and women's cultural image may have been more exalted. But the sex-linked complementarity of work roles established at that time became the basis for an increasingly repressed role and image of women. Each new development of social organization drew activities out of women's place and assigned them to men. Women, once the center of productive economic life, became more and more marginalized, as the place of the home shrank to its present proportions of a purely consumer and child-raising unit. In the primitive struggle for survival it might have seemed "natural" and inevitable that men take the warrior and hunting roles and women manage more sedentary activities. However, because men thereby seized control of what was to become the sphere of political power, the socialization of all power and status was thereby developed at the expense of women. Women's place became a shrinking cage where she was progressively entrapped.

In the rise of civilization, the development of class distinction allowed elite males to manage the collective resources of society for their own benefit. But women of this same group were excluded from these public roles. A male priestly and scribal class monopolized the transmission of culture and banned women from participation. These new leadership and cultural roles were based on no biological advantage of males. Indeed physical strength now became labor to be exploited in a working class, not the real basis of ruling-class power. Women, although lighter in musculature on the average than males, are in no sense biologically inferior, making up in endurance for their lesser weight. The physical advantage that males had over them in the primitive struggle for survival could have become obsolete with the development of civilization. But instead the priestly and scribal classes projected artificial ideologies of male intellectual superiority and female inferiority in the realm of spirit and culture to justify the monopolization of this power in the hands of the male ruling class. The exclusion of women from education meant that each time a skill was professionalized, women were prevented from entering the educational institutions required for it, forbidden to exercise it on the basis of practical experience as, in the case of medicine, they had done before. Thus many skills once exercised by women were progressively taken from their hands.

With these developments women cease to be natural beings whose social existence has a credible relationship to their actual capacities at a given stage of technological organization. Rather, woman becomes "Eve," an unnatural creation of a male ruling class, molded by repression and exclusion into an antidevelopment. Dress, confinement, lack of physical development, direct bodily repression through corsets, footbinding, or veils mold women, especially of the leisured class, into an unnatural physical weakness and psychological timidity. Restricted to a sheltered sphere, kept from education and enlarging experiences, they can scarcely sense in themselves the diminishment of their true potential.

Males, by contrast, are expected to graduate from the home into spheres of training for power and to shape their bodies through sports (the preparation for war) into an aggressive form and self-confident image. The development of technology frees men from biological limitations, while women are prevented from gaining access to technology, especially in the reproductive sphere, that could free them from biological victimization. Ruling-class males preserve and extend a hunter and warrior mystique of maleness into the civilized era, when it should have become obsolete, biasing all the development of culture in the direction of competitive aggressiveness rather than social cooperation. It is perhaps not too much to say that the Achilles' heel of human civilization, which today has reached global genocidal and ecocidal proportions, resides in this false development of maleness through repression of the female.

This discussion of the stages of women's social history may help to explain the puzzling transition from maternal to male-dominated mythic systems, often with the persistence of the mother-centered system underneath the father-centered one. This transition does not represent a change from female political rule to male political rule, for even in matrilineal societies the mother's brother, not the woman, exercises rule. Rather, the mother-goddess symbol represents a society directly interacting and dependent on nature for survival, an experience which persisted for peasant peoples even after the urban revolution. The importance of women in a family-centered economy, the centrality of the mother as life-giver of every child, makes woman the symbol of "nature." This symbolic role of women is gradually repressed or subordinated by a male elite, who begin to rationalize an artificial debilitation of women in more developed social organization, and who begin to feel themselves the masters, rather than the children, of organic nature.

This early image of the woman as nature goddess looked something like this, at least as we find it in myths of ancient Near Eastern peoples of Babylonia and Canaan. The first genesis story is uroboric. The foundation of the cosmos is symbolized as a "world egg" or womb. The cosmos gestates or differentiates into sky and earth, male and female divinities within the primal womb. This concept of genesis does not allow sky and earth to divide into absolute polarities, i.e., "sky" does not symbolize transcendence over against a lower and dependent "earth." The differentiation is complementary, but not hierarchical. Even the gods arise within the primal womb. This view is found in the Babylonian *Genesis*.[4] The younger generations of deities, who have been born from the earth mother and sky father, must defeat the primal mother, Tiamat. Their champion is Marduk, the god-king who defeats the invading primal mother to split up her body into the heaven and the earth, i.e., to re-establish the differentiated cosmos out of her body. The *Ur-*Mother represents a continual threat of collapse back into undifferentiated chaos. But the deities who defeat her are not outside or "above" her, but they subdue and reorder the matrix within which they themselves exist.

As distinct from Tiamat, or the primal mother, the earth goddess represents ordered agricultural nature. She is pictured as siding with the king, but not in a dependent relation to him. Rather, the earth mother and her daughter, the fertility goddess, are seen as powerful, autonomous figures who support the king in order to create ordered civilization. The earth mother, therefore, does not merely represent natural fertility, but she represents both natural fertility and social order or wisdom. In the Canaanite *Ras Shamra* literature the autonomy and energy of the Lady Anath is notable throughout.[5] She is a powerful battle goddess who defeats the enemies of Baal, intercedes for him and rescues him from the powers of drought and death. Finally, she takes the initiative in the sacred marriage. But she does this on his behalf. The male consort reigns, but it is from the mother goddess that his power over natural and social regenerative processes derives and is re-established in his hands.

The relation of the mother goddess to the king is a mother-son relationship. The king is the son of the Great Mother, who grows up to be her consort, in turn producing the "young king" who takes his place. The Egyptian god-king is pictured as enthroned upon the lap of Queen Isis, one of whose titles is the "throne." [6] All power, generative and political, is based on the maternal. Men exercise power by basing themselves upon the Great Mother. Men see themselves as children of the nature mother, created by her, exercising power through worshiping her, rather than transcendent or prior to her. Nevertheless, it is a son, not a daughter, whom the Great Mother installs in power. Thus, although the image of the mother goddess reflects a period when men saw themselves as dependent on nature, rather than potentially its masters, this stage of religious symbols also reflects the first stage of a male cooptation of the female into a system of power exercised by males.

THE NEGATION OF THE MOTHER

Sometime in the early first millennium B.C. there arose, in Hebrew and in Greek cultures, a new stage of consciousness. Parallel developments took place in the axial period of other classical cultures, but we will concentrate on the myths of these two sources of Western culture. In the classical stage of civilization men entertain the possibility of freeing themselves from dependency on nature altogether. They seek to master nature, not by basing themselves on it and exalting it as an independent divine power, but by subordinating it and linking their essential selves with a transcendent principle beyond nature which is pictured as intellectual and male. This image of transcendent, male, spiritual deity is a projection of the ego or consciousness of ruling-class males, who envision a reality, beyond the physical processes that gave them birth, as the true source of their being. Men locate their true origins and natures in this transcendent sphere, which thereby also gives them power over the lower sphere of "female" nature.

In genesis stories created out of this view, the world is no longer seen as evolving out of a primal matrix which contains within it both heaven and earth, the organic and the spiritual. Creation is seen as initiated by a fiat from above, from an immaterial principle beyond visible reality. Nature, which once encompassed all reality, is now subjugated and made the lower side of a new dualism. Anthropology and cosmology are split into a dualism between a transcendent spiritual principle and a lower material reality. A struggle ensues against the old nature and mother religions by prophets or philosophers who portray it as immoral or irrational. Consciousness is abstracted into a sphere beyond visible reality, including the visible heavens. This higher realm is the world of divinity. The primal matrix of life no longer encompasses spiritual power, gods and souls, but is debased as mere "matter" (a word which means "mother").[7] Matter is created by an ego-fiat from a transcendent spiritual power. Visible nature is posterior and created by transcendent "Mind." Sky and earth, once complementary, become hierarchical. Maleness is identified with intellectuality and spirituality; femaleness is identified with the lower material nature. This also defines the female as ontologically dependent and morally inferior to maleness.

This view of women as inherently inferior, servile, and "carnal" beings creates a symbol system which is also applied to the relations of masters and slaves, ruling and subjugated classes and races. Aristotle systematically develops this view of women as the type of the naturally servile person vis-à-vis free Greek males. In his biological and political sciences, free Greek males represent the ruling "reason," which must subjugate the "body people," represented by women, slaves, and barbarians.[8]

In biblical religion and Greek philosophy we find patriarchal reversal myths which are designed to provide the aetiology of this male-dominated, dualistic world-view. In these stories the woman is inferior, posterior, and created by the male or is identified with the bodily world, which is created by a spiritual realm that is identified with the male "essence." In the story of Adam's rib the male is the original human prototype. Reversing natural experience, he is described as giving birth to the woman with the help of a father God.[9] In Aristotle's biology women are denied all generative potency. They are merely the passive incubators of the male seed which provides the entire formative substance of the homunculus. The earlier view, where the procreative power, centered in the mother, incorporated the phallic power into the maternal womb, is reversed in cultural consciousness. Males are normative humanity. Women are defined as secondary and auxiliary beings or as biologically and morally "defective males." Aristotle even believes that every male seed should normatively produce its own image in another male. Females result only through an aberration in which the lower material principle subverts the male formative principle.[10]

A misogynism developed, both in Greek literature and in the later strata of Old Testament and talmudic Judaism. These texts expound the evilness of women and trace the origins of evil in the world to female figures, such as Eve and Pandora (who are probably debased mother-goddess figures).[11] The Jewish tradition expressed its misogynism in language drawn from the patriarchal family, whereas the Greek tradition came to symbolize it in abstract philosophical language. But these two forms of patriarchal hierarchicalism were parallel and began to amalgamate in the Hellenistic period. Christianity fell heir to the fusion.

Menstrual taboos are prominent in classical religious law: Hebrew, Hindu, Zoroastrian, etc. Remnants survive in Christian canon law.[12] These taboos ascribe a demonic character to sexual fluids, primarily female. This concept of uncleanness is used to segregate adult women for most of their lives and forbid them access to male precincts of sacerdotal, political, and educational power. These negative views have been seen as originating in tribal times.[13] However, it is likely that originally these taboos had a different character. Menstrual blood, as the blood of life, was seen as a dangerously sacral substance. The taboos around it had to do with channeling a powerful element. Its debasement from sacrality to uncleanness took place later, as maternal power was denigrated and suppressed culturally.[14]

The development of eschatological and ascetic religion represents the final stage in the suppression of maternal genesis and the elevation of the male self to supernatural status. This development was fed by the apocalypticism of postbiblical Judaism and the dualistic spiritualism of Hellenism. The two trends are not contrary, but parallel. As apocalypticism is de-historicized, especially following the disappointments of the Jewish wars, its dualisms fuse with Greek spiritualism. Jewish mysticism and Christian asceticism both arise in this gnosticizing of Jewish apocalypticism. Ascetic spirituality had conquered mainstream Christianity by the fourth century, despite earlier resistance, and remained the dominant spirituality until the Reformation. In Roman Catholicism its sway has been challenged from within only in the post-Vatican-II era.

In the Greek prototype of this ascetic spirituality, the true self is the reason or soul, which pre-exists the body. It originates in a transcendent world, whence it has fallen into the lower material realm of somatic existence. Salvation consists of lifelong mortification or separation of the spiritual from the bodily and emotive self, freeing the soul to return to its "true home in heaven." As this dualism deepens in Gnosticism, the visible universe comes to be seen as demonic, created through a fall and governed by

diabolic spirits. The Jesus of the Gnostic gospels declares, "I have come to destroy the works of the female"
(the works of sexual feeling and maternity).[15] This view,
never fully accepted into classical Christian cosmology,
nevertheless comes to govern its spirituality.

In the anthropology of Philo and the Church Fathers,
maleness and femaleness are treated as expressions of
this body-soul split. Women are defined as analogous to
body in relation to the ruling mind: either obediently subjugated body (the wife), or sensual bodiliness in revolt
against the governance of reason (the harlot). Women
are assimilated into the definition of sin. The bodily principle is seen as so intrinsically demonic that the high
road to salvation demands the spurning of bodily life altogether for the ascetical virgin state. Sexuality and procreation correspond to the lower realm of corruption, of
coming-to-be-and-passing-away. Redemption demands
the flight from corruptibility, symbolized by procreation,
to the immutable realm, symbolized by virginity. In
unitary spiritual selfhood, beyond sexuality or duality
("neither male nor female"), men and women might be
spiritually equal. Christianity grants women as well as
men the capacity to seek the higher life of virginity. For
women, virginity frees them from the curse of Eve, which
is to bear children in sorrow and to be under the dominion of the husband (Gen. 3:16).

This new concept of spiritual equality between men
and women in virginity was, however, fatally undermined
by its misogynist and sexually repressive presupposi-
tions. Since the carnal realm was regarded as female,
the female virgin must undertake a double repression,
not only of her bodily feelings (necessary for the male ascetic as well), but of her female "nature" as well. The
woman virgin is said to have transcended her female nature and to have been "transformed into a male." By
contrast, asceticism is said to restore the male to his natural "spiritual virility." Far more restrictions are placed

on the female than the male ascetic, indicating to what extent the Church still regards the female, even as nun, as the dangerous embodiment of the "fleshly principle." [16] The theoretical principle of spiritual equality was constantly undermined in practice in the ascetic life. Female nature is defined as intrinsically lacking the higher traits of intellectual and moral virtue and is associated with the lower traits of suppressed carnality. In monastic authors women are even identified with feces, dung, and death. The figure of Frau Welt in medieval cathedrals, a female figure who is speciously fair from the front but behind is crawling with verminous decay, typifies this association of the female with the sphere of corruptibility, from which male spirit must flee for its life.[17]

Christianity typically produces a schizophrenic view of women. Women are split into sublimated spiritual femininity (the Virgin Mary) and actual fleshly women (fallen Eve). The ideals of virginity are exalted into an ethereal realm of "spiritual motherhood," untainted by any contact with the flesh, while actual women are imaged along the lines of feared and repressed "carnality." The cult of the virgin mother arises, not as a solution to, but as a corollary of, the denigration of fleshly maternity and sexuality. Actual sexuality is analized as "dirt," while the repressed libidinal feelings are sublimated in mystical eroticism, expressed by the spiritual sacred marriage of the virgin soul with Christ.[18] The love of the Virgin Mary does not correct but presupposes the hatred of real women.

The culmination of medieval hostility to women can be seen in the outbreak of the witch hunts of the sixteenth and seventeenth centuries—which we will examine in greater detail in Part Two. The antagonisms nurtured by medieval Christianity seemed to culminate in the era from the Black Death through the religious wars. Medieval anti-Semitism also culminated in an era of massacres, expulsions, and segregation. The demonization of women and Jews appears peculiarly parallel, the

Jews imaging the "evil old father" and the witch the "evil old mother." [19] Most of the persecution fell on old widows outside of family authority who made their living by midwifery and herbal medicine, although in Germany a substantial number of the accused were also young girls. In Puritan witch-trial reports, a penchant for "talking back," a characteristic of old age and penurious self-sufficiency, is accounted *ipso facto* proof of demonic associations. Such a woman proved herself thereby a heretic with no regard for the apostolic commandments of silence and submissiveness toward male authority.[20] In the inquisitor's handbook, the *Malleus Maleficarum*, it becomes clear to what extent the tendency to demonic collusion was identified with "female nature." Indeed the very word *fe-minus* was construed as meaning "lacking in faith." [21] It is estimated that over a million women died in the witch hunts of this period, an outbreak of mass paranoia against a helpless group which Norman Cohn believes can only be compared with the Holocaust.[22]

THE SUBLIMATION OF THE MOTHER

As we have noted, the sublimation of the mother arose as the corollary of the repression of physical sexuality and procreation. The Virgin Mary was the antetype of spiritual femininity over against "carnal femaleness." However, it was only in the romantic reaction following the French Revolution that this concept of spiritual femininity became secularized and generalized as a myth about the superior spiritual nature of women. The nineteenth-century romantic image of women as naturally more delicate, moral, spiritual, less sexual than men was compounded of the fusion of Mariology and courtly love with the bourgeois Protestant idealization of marriage and the home. Protestantism rejected monasticism and the superiority of virginity to marriage. It endorsed the patriarchal family of the Old Testament tradition as the normative Christian family. Mariology disappeared as a direct form of theological speculation, although feminine symbols continued to be used for the relation of the self and the Church to God.

However, Protestantism failed to create any new role for women in religion comparable to the Catholic religious order. Public ministry was forbidden to women, since Paul's dictum that women should keep silent was taken as normative. Woman was put back into the traditional status of the subordinated wife of patriarchy, where she is said to "lack a head of her own," to exist primarily for childbearing, and to be under the dominion of her husband. Tirelessly, the Puritan divines trotted out the Adam's-rib story to define female virtues as those of silence, submissiveness, and service.

Yet in vindicating marriage against celibacy, Puritanism began the romanticization of marriage.[23] Catholicism too was influenced by the ideals of the bourgeois family and began to balance its earlier denigration of marriage by applying the image of spiritual femininity, not only to the virgin life, but to "chaste matrimony" as well. The cult of the "Holy Family" began.

These idealized views of women continued to be mixed with the contrary view of women as the carnal type. When intellectual, independent women of the Renaissance and the Enlightenment challenged the stereotype of female docility and invisibility, the paranoid myths of female viciousness continually surfaced. Much of the misogynist literature that poured out from the sixteenth to the twentieth centuries must be seen as a continuous battle to repress the early stirrings of the feminist movement. Some of the *philosophes*, such as Condorçet, included women in the new ideology of "liberty, equality and *fraternity*,"[24] but most found this a scandalous idea. In the aftermath of the French Revolution, when the very fabric of Western civilization seemed to be undermined, European thinkers went scrambling to recover bits and pieces of a threatened social order. The popularization of the mariological tradition of spiritual femininity was an integral part of this reaction. Romanticism sought, simultaneously, to renew human sensibilities through contact with the mystical depths of nature, from which rationalistic man had become alienated, and to compensate for the depersonalized world of industrialism and democracy that threatened the house of patriarchal society. The Victorian cult of True Womanhood was a compensatory ideology fashioned to serve these needs and negations.[25]

The Victorian ideal of Pure Womanhood was essentially a class ideal, forged not only as a bulwark against the industrial world, but also against the revolt of the masses. Its ideal of feminine purity, untainted by sexual feeling, found its compensation in the proliferation of houses of prostitution. Its bourgeois ideal of the frail, lily-white Lady of leisured society had as its unspeakable underpinnings the sweatshops where working-class women labored long hours for slave wages. Middle-class reformism crusaded against these two evils, but was little prepared to see the way its own society was built upon these twin pillars, as surely as the slave quarters were the underpinnings of plantation life. In the American South, sexism and racism intertwined to produce a racist version of the split between the virginal white woman on the pedestal and the sexually exploited black woman in the kitchen.[26]

In the Victorian ideal, marriage is fused with romantic love, and the fusion is sublimated in the mariological tradition of antisexual purity to create a model of the ideal wife and mother who is a fruitful mother yet a lifelong sexual innocent. The immaculate conception and virgin birth become everyday miracles. The fact that mother had sexual intercourse with father was the secret scandal of every Victorian household. Victorian women were kept carefully ignorant of their own biological functions, to the great detriment of their health. The clothing and enforced passivity of their lives had much the same effect. That women were frail creatures who could scarcely stand the strain of real work or real education was taken for granted as a biological fact. The life of leisured women seemed to bear out this myth. Few bothered to notice the contradiction in the lives of working-class women or, for that matter, the household work done by less wealthy middle-class women. In the early twentieth century eminent doctors could still argue that women's limited potency was such that any energy drawn to her brain in education could render her sterile,[27] despite over thirty years of higher education for women. It took one hundred years of continual struggle for women to breach the basic barriers to civil rights and education in Protestant societies, and Catholic societies have been even slower to change.

The romantic myth of feminine purity forged new arguments against women's activities outside the home. The man's world was alleged to be a place of sordid materialism, while woman's purity derived from her seclusion in the "sanctuary" of the home. The Catholic bishops of Massachusetts, in opposing women's suffrage in 1920, declared that for a woman to enter the sphere of politics was tantamount to becoming a "fallen woman." "She gains nothing by that journey. On the other hand, she loses the exclusiveness, respect and dignity to which she is entitled in her home." [28]

The romantic split between moral femininity and materialistic masculinity reversed the earlier typologies. This split, moreover, was typically identified with a split between the home and the world. The material world is now seen as the "real world," the world of hard practical aggressiveness, devoid of sentiment and morality. It is still regarded as the realm of reason, but reason without the qualities of wisdom and reduced to cause-and-effect rationality. This is the work world of the Victorian male, whence he escapes to repair his spirits in the idealized realm of the home, where all moral, spiritual, and interpersonal values are located. Women, having lost most of the productive functions once centered in the home before industrialism, are reduced primarily to consumer, child-raising, and emotive-compensatory functions. A split between the masculine work world and the feminine domestic support system arose that had not existed before in so rigid a form.

Since women are now regarded as the high priestesses of morality and piety vis-à-vis the real world, the split between home and work, the feminine and the masculine, becomes equated with the split between "moral man" and "immoral society." Morality is lodged in the private sphere, symbolized by marriage. The real world of public man is the realm of competitive egoism, where it is "unrealistic" to speak of morality. Religion and morality are privatized and sentimentalized, so as to lose all serious public power. Morality and religion become the realm of the home, of women. Christian virtue is seen as feminine virtue, an idea already prepared by the traditional image of the Church and the soul as feminine in relation to God. Christ himself becomes essentially a mariological figure in nineteenth-century Protestant theology, exhibiting the passive, self-abnegating role in relation to "the Father." Most of all the institutional Church finds itself encapsulated in the same privatized sphere of domesticated virtue where it had traditionally sought to confine women. The clergy function primarily in the sphere of women and are out of place in the "man's world" of power and business, a fact which gives a new twist to the traditional misogynism of the clergy toward women.[29] Art, humanities, higher culture fall victim to the same process. The alienation of woman culminates in the dehumanization of society.

THE LIBERATION OF WOMEN

The women's movement that arose in the 1960s realizes that a civil rights struggle on behalf of women is insufficient, even though remnants of legal discrimination still abound. It is necessary to dig deeper into the psychopathology of the subjugation of women. One must challenge both a concept of work and a concept of the home that divides these into a male-female interdependence. These are both subjective and objective structures. They are forms that condition our psychology and are objectively embodied in our socioeconomic system. These two realities serve to defeat in practice any mere legal changes made in the status of women, since most women in fact cannot take advantage of such opportunities. To put the matter quite simply: work in our society is based on a male workday that presupposes a wife. With few exceptions, women, not having wives and trying to be someone else's wife, soon find themselves incapacitated in this struggle. There can be no liberation of women merely through changes of psychology and de jure opportunities. Mass liberation of women depends on the fundamental restructuring of the socioeconomic relation between work and the domestic support structure. This second phase of the struggle, the reconstruction of the psychology and social roles of men and women, has barely begun.

The nineteenth-century women's movement allowed itself to remain limited to a civil rights and educational struggle. It backed away from a critique of socioeconomic relations and cultural stereotypes of maleness and femaleness. It tried to build a women's movement on the Victorian doctrine of spiritual femininity. They argued that, if women were the morally superior half of the race, they were needed all the more in the public sphere to "moralize" society. But this effort to grasp the enemy's weapons ended in reinforcing traditional stereotypes of "woman's place." [30] The Freudian revolution showed that one could even eroticize the role of the "Lady" without ending her encapsulation. Moreover, feminism, built on the Victorian cult of True Womanhood, capitulated to racist and class arguments in its quest for the vote. The equalitarian argument of its earlier alliance with the anti-slavery movement was abandoned in favor of the covert suggestion that votes for (white middle-class Protestant) women would double the vote of the white middle-class Protestant majority and ensure the hegemony of the traditional elite over the rising tide of blacks, the working class, and immigrants (this at a time when Jim Crow laws were disfranchising the freedman). The women's movement became diverted into a crusade on the side of the status quo. [31]

The language of women's liberation cannot be built out of the uncritical use of any of these traditional materials of male domination. The myths of spiritual femininity are as dangerous as those of denigrated female sexuality. The women's movement is engaged in an effort to reach behind the history of civilization to a lost alternative. It seeks to find the root of the alienation which has created the sexist image of the self and society, human beings and nature, God and humanity in patriarchal religion. This task is profound yet staggeringly immediate, as the evidence pours in that the antagonisms of male chauvinist civilization are rapidly closing off options for alternative forms of development.

We have seen that sexism is rooted in the "war against the mother," the struggle of the transcendent ego to free itself from bondage to nature. Consciousness arose in a one-sided, antagonistic way by making one half of humanity, not the partner in this struggle, but the symbol of the sphere to be transcended and dominated. Each generation of daughters was subjugated to the fate of their mothers without being allowed their own rise to consciousness side by side with their brothers. The psycho-dynamics of self-knowledge have been spurred by negation of, rather than cooperation with, the "other." Each generation of women has been sacrificed to its own children. History has been the holocaust of women.

Originally, the mother appeared all-powerful, and men sought to exercise power by basing themselves on her. But this symbolic power of the mother even then conflicted with the political subordination of women. As the ego of the ruling class grew more confident, it essayed to suppress the mother symbol altogether, claiming to be itself the creator, not the child, of the mother. Even the memory of female potency was suppressed for a dogma of female posteriority and impotency. The memory survived in the negative form of the dangerous uncleanness of "mother blood." Today this élan of transcendence has come full circle. We rediscover ourselves as children of nature, but children capable of destroying the ground under our own feet.

The false response to this realization is romanticism. Here woman again becomes the symbol of the alien other, but in an idealized way. She is to remain "different" in order to nourish the lost depths of the deracinated ego. Like all patriarchal dualisms, romanticism and rationalism reveal themselves to be two sides of the same antagonism, not the solution to the antagonism. Women seek a reconstruction of relationships for which we have neither words nor models: a reconstruction which can give each person the fullness of their being stolen from them by false polarization. The term for this in the women's movement is *androgyny*. But this word itself is formed out of dualistic origins. Authentic relationship is not a relation between two half selves, but between whole persons, when suppression and projection cease to distort the encounter. We seek a new concept of relationships between persons, groups, life systems, a relationship which is not competitive or hierarchical but mutually enhancing.

The ideology of sexism we have seen to have three distinct layers. In the first layer woman is fitted to be the servant and the object-tool of male power. Here she is imaged as body, property, and chattel. Women share this type of inferiorization with other groups who have been reduced to servitude for their labor: lower classes, conquered races.

The second layer of sexist ideology goes beyond objectification to paranoia. The female as body becomes evil, subversive bodiliness or carnality. She is seen as the "witch," allied with demonic forces, ever deceiving and plotting against constituted male authority. Anti-Semitism similarly turned into an ideology of mass paranoia, producing genocidal outbursts of mass murder. Traditional typology also used "black" and "white" as symbols of evil and good, damnation and salvation. During the colonial period this symbolism was transferred to racism, enabling the white man to see in skin color difference a "natural" symbolism of his election and the divine condemnation of the dark-skinned person.[32] During the Jim Crow era this antagonism burst out in mass paranoia, KKK rallies, and barbaric lynchings. These negative images and paranoid outbreaks toward Jews, Negroes, and women should not simply be identified with each other, however. Each has a distinct psychopathology arising from historically and socially distinct types of repressions and contradictions. In the case of women, misogyny is rooted in the specific contradictions of sexual exploitation, i.e., the definition of another person simultaneously as life companion and object of bodily conquest. What is most intimate becomes the arena of subjugation. Ultimately this seems to reflect an abhorrence of one's own body and bodily ties to the generative processes, which the male projects upon the woman. All these make sexism the most central symbol of that distortion of human relations that turns the making of love into the making of war.

Finally we come to a third layer of ideology. Here the

suppressed other is idealized and made into the symbol of the profound depths of mystical "soul power." The dominant class and sexual caste, feeling themselves cut off and alienated from their deeper roots, exalt the other into a mediator of that which they have lost in themselves. Women especially have been used in this romantic way. C. G. Jung has attempted to translate the romantic view of women into a psychoanalytic doctrine. It might be thought that other negated groups, such as blacks, have not been idealized in this way. But the Rousseauan concept of the "noble savage" and the Nazi exaltation of the German peasant similarly made such groups the symbol of lost soul power.[33]

In the recent book by Eulalio Baltazar, *The Dark Center: A Process Theology of Blackness*, there is an effort to reconstruct the symbol of blackness. Instead of being a negative symbol of sin or ignorance, it must become a positive symbol of that profundity of mystical darkness that transcends rationality. The narrowly rationalist white man shunned blackness as an expression of his flight from encounter with his own darker self.[34] It is not clear whether such an explanation of racism is useful. But it should be apparent that liberation theologies constructed on romantic lines, toward either blacks or women, spring from an agenda dictated by the oppressors, not the oppressed. It is the white male who feels himself to have lost his soul and seeks his alienated unconscious by romanticizing women or blacks.

The romantic agenda always suggests that the "noble savages" should remain in their soulful primitivity, so they can nourish what the dominant group has lost. This may give women, blacks, peasants, or Indians a better image, but it leaves them basically where they have always been. This seems to be one reason for the eruption of hostility toward white youths in the civil rights movement in the mid-sixties. Blacks sensed that white youth were parasiting off the black movement to fulfill needs in themselves. This led the black movement down the wrong path, while allowing whites to avoid confronting who they really were. Women similarly must reject any revival of the romantic trap. If white males need to recover their lost soul, women need to recover the rationality, autonomy, and self-definition which they have been denied as tools of male needs and negations. The development of wholeness in each must move in complementarily opposite directions. Only when males, seeking their suppressed unconscious, recognize that they must also help women nurture their suppressed qualities of ego, self-esteem, and rationality can their relationship cease to be parasitical and become genuinely reciprocal.

The analysis of women's liberation must reckon with several different levels of problematics. The first stage of liberation is generally subjective and psychoanalytical. This is the process of raising consciousness, of exorcising debasing self-images projected upon the oppressed and internalized by them. In this case that involves the exploration of the history of sexism and the reconstruction of its ideology in order to loosen its hold on the self and to permit the gradual growth of self-definition over against a world defined in male terms.

The second stage is one of social *praxis*. Here purely individualistic concepts of consciousness are insufficient. One must begin to see the way women as a group are entrapped by the systemic structuring of male-female roles. One must begin to analyze the insufficiency of legal redress, important as this continues to be. One must begin to envision a radically reconstructed society where work and home stand in a different relationship, allowing men and women to participate equally in both spheres, rather than segregating each primarily on one side of the polarization.[35]

Third, women must become self-critical about their own class and racial contexts. Women are not a class or a race. Models of liberation drawn from Marxism or racial liberation are misleading when applied to women. Women must find an analysis of their social condition which is appropriate. Women are sociologically a sexual caste within every class and race. All women share certain common oppressions as women: dependency, secondary existence, domestic labor, sexual exploitation, and the structuring of their role in procreation into a total definition of their existence. There is, in this sense, a common condition of women in general. But women are also divided against each other by their integration into oppressor and oppressed classes and races. This makes the protest of the middle-class American white woman, in rebellion against the stifling horizons of bedroom suburbia, very different from the poor Indian woman of the Latin American *favela* on the bottom of the hierarchies of class, race, and sex. Women of oppressed classes and races cannot separate their struggle as women from their struggle as poor people of oppressed races. Rather, they must seek to lead their class and racial struggle out beyond the limits of patriarchal concepts of liberation.

However, women of the upper class and race easily fall into an abstract analysis of woman's "oppressed status" that ignores their own class and race privileges. When this happens, their movement fails to connect with that of women of oppressed groups. Their movement becomes a white upper-class movement, which fails to go beyond the demand for privileges commensurate with those enjoyed by males of their group, oblivious to the unjust racist and class context of these privileges. The women's movement can avoid becoming a white upper-class movement only if it constantly seeks an awareness and social *praxis* that exposes the bourgeois image of the "Lady," not only as a sexist, but as a racist and class doctrine as well. The women's movement in the dominant society must seek conversation with black and third world women, so they can understand the different agenda of feminism among those seeking to bring their class and racial struggle beyond patriarchalism.[36] They must analyze the contradictions between these two brands of feminism and seek ways of overcoming these contradictions in mutual support. Only this cooperation can save the women's movement from the covert class and racist bias which overtook the latter stages of the old women's movement of the nineteenth and early twentieth centuries.

Fourth, our vision of a new society of social justice must reckon with the ecological crisis. Nineteenth-century progressivism imagined that disadvantaged peoples could gradually be included in the privileges hitherto reserved for the ruling class by the infinite expansion of production. This concept of infinite expansion was deeply rooted in one version of patriarchal theology. In nineteenth-century thought, the infinite transcendent God of patriarchy was incarnated into his historical process to create a vision of an expanding future of infinite horizons. Today we recognize that infinite material demand inflicted on a finite earth is rapidly destroying the ground under our feet.

If women and oppressed classes and races are not to be cheated of their future in a world of dwindling resources, hoarded by the present power holders, we must seek the fundamental reconstruction of the way resources are allocated within the world community. This implies a fundamental reconstruction of our basic model of interrelationships between persons, social groups and, finally, between humans and nature. Our model of relationships must cease to be hierarchical and become mutually supportive, a cooperative model of fellowship of life systems. As Vine Deloria says, in his Indian liberation theology, *God Is Red,* we must believe, not just in the brotherhood of man, but in the fellowship of life.[37] Or, as Mary Daly declares, we must seek, not just the new social covenant, but the new cosmic covenant as well.[38]

Notes

1. *The Early Development of the Family (from The Origins and History of the Family, Private Property and the State*, Zurich, 1884). New England Free Press pamphlet, p. 66.
2. Rt. Rev. Kilmer C. Meyers to the clergy convention of California, October 1971, reprinted in *Christianity and Crisis* XXXI, No. 21 (Dec. 13, 1971), pp. 275–76.
3. J. J. Bachofen, *Myth, Religion and Mother Right* (1861) (Princeton: Princeton University Press, 1967); R. Briffault, *The Mothers: The Matriarchal Theory of Social Origins* (1927) (New York: Grosset and Dunlap, 1963); L. H. Morgan *Ancient Society* (1877) (Cambridge, Mass.: Harvard University Press, 1965). Popular feminist presentations of the thesis are found in Helen Diner, *Mother and Amazons: The First Feminist History of Culture* (first published in Germany, 1929) (Garden City, N.Y.: Doubleday, 1973), and E. G. Davis, *The First Sex* (New York: Putnam, 1972).
4. *Religions of the Ancient Near East: Sumero-Akkadian Religious Texts and Ugaritic Epics*, ed. Issac Mendelsohn (New York: Liberal Arts Press, 1955), pp. 17–46.
5. A. S. Kapelrud, *The Violent Goddess: Anath in the Ras Shamra Texts* (Oslo: Universitetsforlaget, 1969).
6. See fig. 4, "Isis with the King," Temple of Seti I, Abydos, XIX dynasty, from Erich Neumann, *The Great Mother* (Princeton: Princeton University Press, 1963). The Isis-Horus figure was the iconographical prototype of the Christian image of Mary seated with the baby Jesus, with insignia of kingship, in her lap. Cf. G. Miegge, *The Virgin Mary* (Toronto: Ryerson, 1955), p. 75.
7. Plato, *Timaeus* 50–51, where matter is called "the mother."
8. Plato developed concepts of transcendent spirituality and flight from the body in the *Phaedo* and the *Phaedrus*, but only occasionally correlates it with ontological inferiority of women, i.e., *Timaeus* 91. In Aristotle, the correlation of women/carnality is standard: *Politics* I: 1–2, and *On the Generation of Animals* I: 729b; II: 731b, 737a, 738b.
9. Theodore Reik, *The Creation of Woman* (New York: McGraw-Hill, 1960), p. 83.

10. See n. 8, above. This definition of woman as a misbegotten male is standard in medieval scholasticism. Cf. Aquinas, *Sum. Theo.*, Q. 99, Art. 2, I, 92.

11. Katherine Rogers, *The Troublesome Helpmate: A History of Misogyny in Literature* (Seattle, University of Washington Press, 1966), pp. 11–14, 22–37.

12. Clara Maria Henning, "Canon Law and the Battle of the Sexes," in *Sexism and Religion: Images of Women in the Jewish and Christian Traditions*, ed. R. Ruether (New York: Simon and Schuster, 1974), p. 273.

13. H. R. Hays, *The Dangerous Sex: The Myth of Feminine Evil* (New York: Pocket Books, 1972), chaps. 1–6.

14. This thesis has been developed by Emily Culpepper in papers on menstruation taboos in Jewish law (presented at the New England regional American Academy of Religion (A.A.R.) conference, Spring (1973) and on Zoroastrian menstrual taboos, presented at the annual A.A.R. conference, Chicago, November 1973; published in *Women and Religion*, ed. J. A. Romero (American Academy of Religion, 1973), pp. 94–103. The debilitation expected of women because of menstruation in the Victorian era can be seen in M. Vicinus, *Suffer and Be Still: Women in the Victorian Era* (Bloomington: Indiana University Press, 1972), pp. 38ff.

15. *Gospel of the Egyptians*, from Clement of Alexandria, *Strom.* III, 9, 63.

16. R. Ruether, "Misogynism and Virginal Feminism in the Fathers of the Church," in *Sexism and Religion*. For the background of this anthropology in Hellenistic Judaism, see R. Baer, *Philo's Use of the Categories of Male and Female* (Leiden: Brill, 1972).

17. Eleanor McLaughlin, "Equality of Souls: Inequality of Sexes: Women in Medieval Thought," in *Sexism and Religion*, pp. 253–54.

18. The allegorical interpretation of the Song of Songs as the love between Yahweh and Israel was established in rabbinic commentary in the first century A.D. (chap. 2, below, n. 13). Origen's commentary on it established the Christian mystical interpretation as the sacred marriage between Christ and the soul. In commentaries by Bernard of Clairvaux, William of Thierry, and many others this tradition continued through medieval mysticism.

19. J. Trachtenberg, *The Devil and the Jews* (New Haven: Yale University Press, 1943), pp. 207–16; also T. S. Szasz, *The*

Manufacture of Madness (New York: Harper & Row, 1970), p. 8.

20. Leo Bonfanti, *The Witchcraft Hysteria of 1692* (New England Historical Publications, 1971), pp. 10, 33, and *passim.*

21. Barbara Yoshioka, "The Female Witch and the Female Sectarian Preacher," presented at the annual A.A.R. meeting, Chicago, 1973; published in *Women and Religion*, pp. 56ff.; see also Walter H. Wagner, "The Demonization of Women," *Religion in Life* (Spring 1973), pp. 71ff.

22. Norman Cohn, *Warrant for Genocide: The Myth of the Jewish World Conspiracy and the Protocols of the Elders of Zion* (New York: Harper & Row, 1966), p. 17.

23. Wm. and M. Haller, "The Puritan Art of Love," *Huntington Library Quarterly*, 5: 235–71.

24. "Condorçet's plea for the Citizenship of Women" (1798), *The Fortnightly*, 17 (1870): 719–29; see also John Stuart Mill, *The Subjugation of Women* (1869), classical liberal principles applied to the equality of women.

25. R. Ruether, "The Cult of True Womanhood and Industrial Society," *Commonweal* (Nov. 9, 1973), pp. 127–32.

26. Ann Gordon, Mari Jo Buhle, and Nancy Schrom, "Women in American Society," *Radical America*, V, 4 (July–August 1971); see also Anne Firor Scott, *The Southern Lady: From Pedestal to Politics. 1830–1930* (Chicago: Chicago University Press, 1970), chap. 1.

27. R. Ruether, "Are Women's Colleges Obsolete?" in *The Critic* (October–November 1968), pp. 58–64.

28. "Cardinal Gibbons Says Women Should Keep from the Polls," Documents of the Catholic Bishops of Massachusetts against Women Suffrage, 1916–1920, Sophia Smith Collection, Smith College, Northampton, Massachusetts.

29. R. Ruether, "Male Clericalism and the Dread of Women," *The Ecumenist*, XI, No. 5 (July–August 1973), pp. 65–69.

30. William O'Neill, "Feminism as a Radical Ideology," in *Dissent*, ed. Alfred Young (De Kalb, Ill.: Northern Illinois University Press, 1968); see also William O'Neill, *Everyone Was Brave* (Chicago: Quadrangle Books, 1969), pp. 295ff.

31. Aileen Kraditor, *The Ideas of the Women's Suffrage Movement, 1890–1920* (Garden City, N.Y.: Doubleday, 1971), chaps. 3, 6, 7.

32. Eulalio Baltazar, *The Dark Center: A Process Theology of Blackness* (New York: Paulist Press, 1973), chap. 3.

33. George Mosse, *The Crisis of German Ideology* (New York: Grosset and Dunlap, 1964), pp. 52–87.

34. Baltazar, *op. cit.*, chaps. 7–9.

35. Juliet Mitchell, "Women: The Longest Revolution," in B. and T. Roszak, eds., *Masculine/Feminine* (New York: Harper & Row, 1969), pp. 160–72.

36. Joyce Ladner, *Tomorrow's Tomorrow: The Black Woman* (Garden City, N.Y.: Doubleday, 1971); see also Gerda Lerner, *Black Women in White America* (New York: Random House, 1972), pp. 587–92, and *passim*.

37. Deloria, *God Is Red* (New York: Grosset and Dunlap, 1973), p. 103.

38. Daly, *Beyond God the Father* (Boston: Beacon Press, 1973), pp. 155ff.

Mistress of Heaven:
The Meaning of Mariology

IN 1974 POPE PAUL VI PROPOSED THAT CHRISTIANITY AL-
ready had a model of the liberated woman in the Virgin
Mary.[1] Although few feminists are likely to respond to the
figure of Mary because the Pope told them to, nevertheless women, Protestants as much as Catholics, are taking a second look at Mariology to see what positive content for women might exist in this solitary feminine
symbol in what appears otherwise a solidly patriarchal
religion. Some years ago the Protestant theologian Paul
Tillich suggested that Protestantism was too one-sidely
masculine and needed some of the balancing elements
of the feminine symbols that existed in Catholicism.[2] The
psychologist C. G. Jung hailed the doctrine of the assumption of Mary as the symbolic reintegration of the
fatal polarities in Western consciousness between masculine and feminine, body and spirit, earth and heaven.[3]

In her book *Beyond God the Father*, Mary Daly rejects
Christology as a redemptive symbol for women, but suggests that redemptive content can be found in a new
look at mariological doctrines. Mary's virginity can be understood as the symbol of female autonomy, her com-
pleteness and integrity in herself, apart from the male.
The doctrine of the immaculate conception counteracts
the myth of woman as Eve, the cursed source of sin. Im-
maculately conceived woman is woman without sin,
good in her true, created nature. She is woman as norm
of perfected and authentic humanity. The assumption
overcomes the hierarchical split between soul and body,
male and female. It reintegrates humanity as androgynous personhood and redeemed body.[4]

36

Yet despite these liberating possibilities of Mariology, feminists also realize that it is churches with a high Mariology which are most negative to women. It is the Protestant churches without Mariology which ordain women. Mariology operates socially as a right-wing rallying cry among Catholics. It is used as a way of condemning the liberal personal and political mores of the "modern world." Mariology, as it is used by the clergy, seems antithetical to the liberation of women. Whose side is Mary on?

THE PREBIBLICAL SOURCES OF MARIOLOGY

Just as Christianity inherited and transformed the ancient Near Eastern concept of the messianic god-king, so Mariology gathers up, in a transformed way, the Queen of Heaven and virgin mother of Mediterranean religion. Since both symbols were mediated to the Church through Judaism, the prebiblical origins of Christ and Mary were not recognized.

The mother-goddess symbol exists in a plurality of forms. Its meaning changes considerably in different stages of development. In the preceding chapter I have noted two kinds of female god symbols. First there is a female symbol for genesis or creation itself. The "ground of being" is envisioned as a divine matrix or world egg within which heaven and earth, gods and humans differentiate. Creation takes place within the womb of the *Ur*-Mother, who must also be defeated and subjected to order. Second, there is the Great Mother or nature goddess who stands for ordered unity of humans and nature in agricultural civilization. The Great Mother represents not just "nature," in the sense of natural fecundity, but also wisdom and law. She is the power of life and its ordered rebirth, upon whose lap the god-king sits as King of Creation. The Great Mother is both a bride and mother and also a virgin. Her maidenhood symbolizes her ever-renewed pristine youth. It also indicates her self-directing autonomy. But there is a tendency for the image to split into two, with the Great Mother receding behind the sister-bride, the maiden-wife of the god-king.[5]

In Greek mythology a further development has taken place. The various aspects of the mother goddess—the huntress, the warrior maiden, the love goddess, and the mother goddess—all originally joined as aspects of the Great Mother, have split into separate female figures: Artemis, Athena, Aphrodite, and Hera. Greek myth reveals a certain hostility to the goddess in her maternal aspect. Hera is reduced to the nagging, petulant wife of Zeus, perhaps reflecting the negative relation to the wife and mother that developed in classical Greece.[6] The most powerful and awesome female figures are virgin goddesses, Artemis and Athena. Athena especially combines the attributes of wisdom and the warrior maiden who rescues the Hero. Athena, patroness of Athens, is totally male identified, being herself reborn from the head of father Zeus. In Aeschylus' *Oresteia*, Athena casts the deciding vote in favor of father right over mother right, banishing the blood spirits of the murdered mother to inferior status.[7] In the war of patriarchy to suppress mother right, the virgin warrior is separated from the Great Mother and allied with the rule of the father. She renounces sexuality and maternity and the vindication of the blood rights of the female. She is no longer the virgin mother, but a virgin, not mother.

There is yet a fifth stage of development of the female symbols that can be discerned in antiquity. After the Greek conquest of the Persian empire, the ancient fertility religions begin to lose their connections with their original tribal locus. Originally they were the public religions of particular societies, centered in the temple of the leading city, led by the king, whereby the community as a whole participated in the annual rites of renewal. With the loss of political autonomy of these nations, their religions become private rites of initiation of individuals. But, at the same time, they become missionary religions which spread throughout the empire, open to all nations. The rites of renewal change their meaning as well. Instead of just celebrating a this-worldly renewal of the earth and society, they have become eschatological religions. The mysteries of the death and rebirth of the vegetation god and the earth mother have now become the path of redemption of the soul to life after death. The mother-goddess figure grows more dominant, probably because of the loss of the political basis of god-kingship for the male consort. In the mysteries of Isis, Osiris is almost eclipsed. A new asceticism and spirituality comes to characterize her worship. The priests of Isis are celibate, tonsured, and dressed in white linen. Fasting, prayer, and moral renewal precede initiation into her mysteries. She appears to her devotees as the Queen of Heaven of shining purity, crowned with the moon and garlanded with stars, fruits, and flowers:

> Behold me, Lucius, moved by thy prayers. I am the Mother of Nature, Mistress of all the elements, first Progenetrix of the ages, Supreme among the divinities, Queen of the dead, First of celestial beings, Figure alike of Gods and Goddesses. With my nod I govern the heights of heaven in their brightness, the healthbringing winds of the sea, the mournful silences of the underworld. My divinity in its uniqueness is worshipped by all the world in many forms, by various rites, under divers names. The Phrygians, first born among the peoples, call me Mother of the Gods of Pessinus; the autochthonous Athenians, Minerva Cecrops; the islanders of Cyprus, Venus Paphia; the Cretans who draw the bow, Diana Dictynna; the Sicilians who speak three tongues, Stygian Proserpina; the Eleusinians, the ancient Goddess Ceres; some call me Juno, others Bellona, Hecate, Ramnusia. The Ethiopians, lighted by the first rays of the rising sun and the Arii, and the Egyptians, wise through ancient lore, honor me with rites that are proper to me and call me by my true name, Isis Regina.[8]

The goddess instructs Lucius in the way to seek initiation into her mysteries. Through repentance he will experience the true birthday of his soul and win release from his evil enchantment and also assurance of life after death.

> Under my protection you will be happy and famous, and when, at the destined end of your life . . . from the Elysian Fields you will see me as Queen of the profound Stygian realm . . . if you are found to deserve my divine protection by careful obedience to the ordinances of my religion and by perfect chastity, you will become aware that I, and I alone have the power to prolong your life beyond the limits appointed by destiny.[9]

In the mystery religions the Great Mother of springtime resurrection becomes the mother of eschatological resurrection of the soul to life everlasting. Instead of commanding mankind to release their fertility as a sacrament of earthly blessing, she orders them to repress it as the means to the higher life. In this eschatological transformation of the goddess in antiquity we seem to see the cultural counterparts in late Greco-Roman religion to what will be the dominant meaning of the virgin mother in Christianity. The virgin mother of Christ and the virgin Church, mother of reborn souls, is no longer earth mother, but eschatological mother. Not sexuality, but virginity is the means to rebirth to the higher life.

THE TRANSFORMATION
OF THE GODDESS IN ISRAEL

Old Testament religion is usually presented as an uncompromising war against nature religion, as represented by the cult of Baal and Anath. The assumption has made us fail to discern the extent to which the psalms and prophets have assimilated, in a transformed way, the cultic language and vision of the transfiguration of nature. Nature and society are not divorced in their account of the relation of God and humanity, but form an interconnected realm which falls into chaos with God's wrath and the apostasy of the people, and is revived to paradisiacal harmony with the return of the people to obedience and the advent of God. Hidden behind the messianic language of the psalms and prophets is a remarkable adaptation of the nature renewal pattern in moral-historical terms.[10] The Yahwists sought to drive out Baal as god-king of the conquered land. But, for popular piety, this meant that Yahweh became instead the consort of the Great Mother. Ashtaroth was worshiped in the Solomonic temple for more than half of its duration. Indeed a temple cultus, psalms, kingship, and annual festivals were all adapted by Israel from Canaan. As Raphael Patai has shown in his book *The Hebrew Goddess*, Ashtaroth survives in hidden ways in Old Testament thought, and surfaces again as symbol of Mother Israel and the feminine dimension of God in talmudic and kabbalistic traditions.[11]

But within the Old Testament the image of the goddess is so suppressed that it can emerge only in a very chastened and transformed way. The spouse of Yahweh is no longer the Great Mother, who encompasses her son-lover, but the people Israel, whom the Father God creates and elects as his bride. Indeed this idea of Israel as daughter-bride of Yahweh appears only dimly in the Hebrew Scriptures. Hosea is the one who primarily develops this motif. But even he can use the image only in a negative way.[12] Israel is a wayward bride who plays the harlot with Baal, with whom she apparently had a friskier relationship and to whose embraces she keeps returning, disobedient to the stern commandments of her new Lord. To portray the covenant of God and Israel as a marriage relationship transforms the Canaanite sacred marriage into Hebrew patriarchy. But the struggle against nature religion is too immediate for the image to be used in other than judgmental terms: Israel as unfaithful bride, harlot of Baal. Yet the Rabbis also enshrined the adapted hymn to the sacred marriage, the Song of

Songs, defending its place in the canon by declaring that it was the very "Holy of Holies of Scripture." The identities of the bride and her lover were none other than Israel and God.[13]

In talmudic thought the idea of Israel as bride of Yahweh is developed in a new way. The Shekinah (God's presence) is also Mother Israel. She is God's beloved but estranged wife. The exile represents an estrangement between God and his people. But although God has withdrawn into heaven, his bride, the Shekinah, remains with Israel and goes with them into exile. After the holy celebration of the Sabbath, the pious embrace of husband and wife represents a reconciliation of God and his Shekinah. The Sabbath hymn hails the advent of the Sabbath Queen, the redeemed bridal Israel. The Shekinah is both the collective representation of Israel as bride and mother and also the immanent presence of God among the people.[14]

FEMININE SYMBOLS IN CHRISTIAN THEOLOGY

Christianity inherited and developed this use of feminine symbols in Israel. In Christianity feminine symbols appear as expressions of three types of theological relationships. The primary function of the feminine image is ecclesiological. The community, Israel or the Church, is represented as bride of God or bride of Christ and mother of the faithful. Since Christianity regards itself as the obedient and redeemed bride of Christ, over against Israel, the faithless people and rejected bride, the critical aspect of the symbol is suppressed. The Church cannot be admitted to be a harlot or even an estranged bride. She is the bride without spot or wrinkle of the eschatological nuptials of the new Jerusalem:

> . . . Christ loved the church and gave himself up for her, that he might sanctify her, having cleansed her by the washing of water with the word, that the church might be pre-

sented before him in splendor, without spot or wrinkle or any such thing, that she might be holy and without blemish. (Ephesians 5:25–27)

Their union is not complete. In the book of Revelation, the Church is a suffering, persecuted pregnant woman, who flees before the dragon into the wilderness, bearing the birth pangs of the messianic people (Rev. 12). But one also sees her through the eyes of the future redemption:

And I saw the holy city, new Jerusalem, coming down out of heaven from God, prepared as a bride adorned for her husband. (Revelation 21:2)

The second major function of feminine symbols in Jewish and Christian theology is sophiological, i.e., the feminine aspect of God, God's self-disclosure or immanence. The feminine gender of several of these words in Hebrew (*ruah*, "spirit"; *shekinah*, "presence") and also in Greek (*sophia*, "wisdom") suggested this feminine personification. In Latin *spiritus* was masculine, masculinizing the third person of the Trinity, but *sapientia* was feminine and so continued the sophia tradition applied to Mary. But behind this personification of wisdom as a feminine expression of God lurks the tradition of the Great Mother who is wisdom. The daughter of God who springs from his head as the expression of his wisdom was already found in the Athena story. In the Hellenistic Jewish and Greek Christian sophiological tradition, Sophia is a feminine parallel of the Logos. Sophia is the daughter of God who is seated at his right hand, through whom he creates the world, who governs the world as God's providence, who reveals God to humanity and through whom the souls of the wise are led into communion with God. She is the agent of God in creation, providence, revelation, and redemption.

I will tell you what wisdom is and how she came to be, ... For she is a breath of the power of God, and a pure emanation of the glory of the Almighty; therefore nothing defiled gains entrance into her. For she is a reflection of eternal light, a spotless mirror of the working of God, and an image of his goodness. Though she is but one, she can do all things, and while remaining in herself, she renews all things; in every generation she passes into holy souls and makes them friends of God, and prophets; . . . She reaches mightily from one end of the earth to the other, and she orders all things well. I loved her and sought her from my youth, and I desired to take her for my bride, and I became enamored of her beauty. . . . With thee is wisdom, who knows thy works and was present when thou didst make the world, and who understands what is pleasing in thy sight and what is right according to thy commandments. Send her forth from the holy heavens, and from the throne of thy glory send her, that she may be with me and toil, and that I may learn what is pleasing to thee. (Wisdom of Solomon 6:22; 7:25–27; 8:1–2; 9:9–10)

In Proverbs the Jewish mother who guides her sons in righteousness is the manifestation of God's wisdom. Wisdom is, so to speak, the heavenly Jewish mother, mediating the will of the Father to the children of Israel.

Eastern Christianity developed sophiology as a theological theme. Here it can be seen, not only as an expression of the Word or Spirit of God, but it can even be read as the encompassing divine power which governs the whole process by which God is revealed, created the world, guides it to perfection, and encompasses the redeemed cosmos and Church in the eschatological community. In Sergius Bulgakov's study *The Wisdom of God*, Sophia is said to be the very *ousia* of God. Sophia is the matrix out of which the three *hypostaseis*—Father, Son, and Spirit—arise. She is that Being of God that also comes forth to become the Ground of Being of the created cosmos, the foundation of the image of God in creation and humanity, the essence of renewed godmanhood in Christ. She is the eschatological feminine present in the Church, who is the foretaste of that final perfection of mankind told in the prophecy of Jeremiah that "the female overcomes the warrior" (Jer. 31:22) which will unite God and creation in the final community of the new heaven and the new earth.[15] She is manifest in the maternity of Mary, whose full meaning is understood only in the light of Holy Wisdom. Bulgakov puts aside the doctrines of the immaculate conception and the assumption, and yet declares that full godmanhood is found, not in Jesus alone, but only in Jesus encompassed by Mary, who together reveal the Word of God completed by the redeemed plentitude of Creation.

> In Her is realized the idea of Divine Wisdom in the creation of the world. She is Divine Wisdom in the created world. In her that Divine Wisdom is justified and thus the veneration of the Virgin blends with that of Holy Wisdom. In the Virgin there are united Holy Wisdom and the wisdom of the created world, the Holy Spirit and the created hypostasis. Her body is completely spiritual and transfigured. She is the justification, the end, the meaning of creation. She is, in this sense, the glory of the world. In her God is already all in all.[16]

The third function of feminine symbols in Christianity is to represent the *psyche* or soul in relation to God, in mystical contemplation and communion. The soul or mind is normally imaged as masculine in relation to the body. In this the relation of mind to body parallels the relation of God to bodily creation and is another analogue of male headship over female bodiliness. However, when the soul is considered in relation to God, it is seen in its passive, receptive aspect, open and receptive to the Word of God and the workings of the Spirit. The soul becomes Virgin Psyche, the bridal soul who awaits the coming of its bridegroom, Christ.

As we have seen, at least by the late second century, with Origen's commentary on the Song of Songs, Christianity had established this Old Testament marriage hymn as the text for the mystical nuptials of the soul with Christ.[17] Throughout the Middle Ages the monastic tradition produced sermons, meditations, and commentaries on the Song of Songs as its scriptural key to mystical communion with God. This writing legitimated a powerful erotic imagery in the heart of mystical theology. The Song of Songs is also the one Scripture written from the feminine side. The speaker of the Song is the woman who longs for her lover, searches for him, anticipates his coming; "O that his left hand were under my head and that his right hand embraced me!" (8:3). Every Christian mystic in relation to God took on, then, a feminine *persona* in relation to the divine lover. This is as true for John of the Cross as for Teresa of Ávila.[18]

THE EVOLUTION OF MARIOLOGICAL DOCTRINE

Mary, the mother of Jesus, was to become the personal figure around whom all these types of feminine images in the theological tradition were to be gathered together. In Latin theology the ecclesiological and mystical modes predominate, while, at least officially, the idea of a feminine aspect of God was not allowed. Despite its exaltation of language, Mary remains a symbol of the self and the community in relation to God, or a maternal mediator between the patriarchal Lord of Heaven and the faithful of the Church. She is not a feminine divine hypostasis. The key mariological doctrines are Mary as the new Eve, her perpetual virginity, her divine maternity, her bodily assumption into heaven, Mary as the mediatrix of all graces, and her immaculate conception.

The New Testament spends little time on Mary as a figure in herself. Even her virginity, in the nativity narratives of Luke and Matthew, is in the context of christological, not mariological, interests. The focus is the virgin birth of Jesus. The virgin birth, theologically, means that the advent of Christ is solely the work of God and is not produced by the works of man (males). Christ, divine grace, comes from above, and is not the product of human history. Since the focus was christological, it could coexist for several centuries with the tradition that Mary, after Jesus' birth, had natural children. The brothers and sisters of Jesus, mentioned various places in the Gospels, Acts, and Paul, were recognized in the early Church as natural siblings of Jesus. One of these, James, the Lord's brother, became the leader of the Jerusalem community.[19] Matthew's Gospel clearly assumes a normal married sexual life of Mary and Joseph after Jesus' birth (Matt. 1:25).

Aside from the nativity stories, Mary appears in the synoptics only in the pejorative scene where she and the brothers come to speak to Jesus, apparently trying to persuade him to leave his preaching and return home. The family of Jesus are presented in the Gospels as nonbelievers, and Jesus responds by repudiating his natural family for his spiritual brothers and sisters. The Marys of the synoptic crucifixion stories are Mary Magdalene and apparently Mary the mother of James the Younger, rather than Jesus' mother, as are the Marys of the resurrection stories. Only John includes Mary, Jesus' mother, at the crucifixion, in a story that established John as Jesus' heir. Mary also appears in John's story of the marriage feast of Cana, again to be somewhat rebuked for making a presumptuous request. Acts includes Mary and the brothers at Pentecost, showing that they were known to be believers in the early Jerusalem community. At what point they enter the believing community from their status of unbelievers during Jesus' ministry is not made known. Nevertheless it is clear that the early historical tradition did not exalt Mary. The feminine figure closest to Jesus was Mary Magdalene. The exaltation of the image of a close relationship between Jesus and his mother in the later tradition has had the effect of suppressing in Christian memory this relationship of Jesus with his female friends and disciples, especially Mary Magdalene, who in all four Gospels is the central female figure of the resurrection stories.[20] Mother Mary is not mentioned in Paul or the other New Testament writings. The dramatic image of the woman in Revelation 12 stands for the Church, although its imagery, drawn from the Isis tradition of the Queen of Heaven, would later be applied to Mary.

The first development of a theological meditation on Mary is found in the Fathers of the later second century, Justin, Tertullian, and Irenaeus. They develop the idea of Mary as the new Eve. The motif comes from the Lukan annunciation story where Mary responds to the angel with the words, "be it done to me according to thy word" (1:37). The hymns of praise which follow have no counterpart in the other nativity story in Matthew. As the new Eve Mary represents the Church. She is the mother or first representative of the new faithful people, the new Israel, who obey the word of God, in contrast to Eve, the mother of fallen humanity, who rejected God's commandment.[21] But there is no real interest in Mariology in the pre-Nicene Fathers.

It is only with the triumph of asceticism in the late fourth century that interest in Mary as a symbol and source of sermons, hymns, and theological reflections begins to be evident in high theology, although the apocryphal infancy narratives suggest an earlier popular interest in Mary.[22] Mary now becomes a central symbol of the ideal of virginity. It becomes necessary to suppress the early traditions of natural children of Mary and Joseph in order to assert that Mary remained a perpetual virgin. Jerome particularly develops the biblical exegesis to defend this thesis. His foes are two monks, Jovinian and Helvidius, who put forth the earlier views of Mary's normal married life and motherhood in order to affirm that marriage and celibacy both have equal merit as paths of virtue. This view was unthinkable to Jerome, who, in a highly polemical treatise, defended the perpetual virginity of Mary and the superiority of virginity over marriage by explaining away the brothers of Jesus as "cousins." [23] Jerome's position became the future tradition of the Church. Jesus also is pictured as a virgin ascetic. This probably was a primary reason for eliminating the tradition of his friendship with Mary Magdalene. The normal sexuality of both Mary and Jesus becomes suppressed, so they can stand for the ideal of chastity untainted by the flesh.

The next major struggle over Mariology took place in the first half of the fifth century over the title *Theotokos* or Mother of God. The title was used by Athanasius, but did not have general currency outside Egypt. The historical school of exegesis of Antioch, represented by Theodore of Mopsuestia and Nestorius, his pupil and bishop of Constantinople in A.D. 428, preferred *Christotokos* to make clear that Mary was the mother of Jesus in his humanity, not the mother of the divine Logos that dwelt in him. The title Mother of God suggested dangerous superiority to God. It also was reminiscent of the title Mother of the Gods of the ancient mother goddesses. Theologically, the argument was over the nature of the consubstantiality of the Word with the Father and the relation of the human and divine natures of Christ.

Could one allow these distinctions to be confused in such a way as to speak of Mary as Mother of God? For the theologians of Antioch such a title dangerously confused these distinctions. Overriding these objections, the Antiochene tradition came to be rejected as heretical. The Christology of Alexandria triumphed in the definition of the *Theotokos* in the Council of Ephesus in A.D. 431, despite its partial defeat at Chalcedon in A.D. 451. The Council of Ephesus declared that in the incarnation the humanity of Jesus has been absorbed into divinity so intimately that it is appropriate to speak of Mary, not just as his mother after the flesh, but as Mother of God.[24] The emotion behind this dispute, however, indicates that more was at stake than a fine point of Christology. The title *Theotokos* represents an opening for the development of popular devotion to Mary as a substitute mother goddess.

Devotion to Mary began to develop rapidly in Egypt in the later fourth century. It was supported by the monks for whom Mary was the symbol of ascetic spirituality and the feminine virgin soul in its openness to God. But it also arose on a popular level as a way of reinstating, through Mary, the popular veneration of the ancient Queen of Heaven. The titles, temples, and iconography of the mother goddesses were transferred to Mary. Many a traditional temple or site of worship was simply rededicated to Mary. The traditional image of Isis with the baby god-king Horus seated in her lap was renamed as a representation of Mary and baby Jesus and became the iconographical source of this favorite image in Christianity.[25] Mariology develops on two levels. There is the Mary of the monks, who venerate her primarily as virgin and shape her doctrines in an antisexual mold. But there is the Mary of the people who is still the earth mother and who is venerated for her power over the secrets of natural fecundity. It is she who helps the woman through her birthpangs, who assures the farmer of his new crops, new rains, and new lambs. She is the maternal image of the divine who understands ordinary people in their wretchedness. Although we are concerned in this chapter primarily with the doctrines developed by the official tradition, we must not forget that the popular base for this devotion is fueled by the second type of piety.

It was from Egypt that the popular doctrine of the bodily assumption of Mary into heaven developed, probably also in the late fourth or early fifth centuries, and began to spread thence north and westward. There are two different versions of the apocryphal story of Mary's death. In the earlier story of the dormition, still preserved in Orthodox piety, Mary's body is carried away by angels, to be buried in an unknown spot until the general resurrection, and her soul is carried up to heaven.[26] As such the story says nothing special about Mary different from other Christians except to make it the focus of a pious meditation on a soul especially beloved by God. There is a second version of the story, however, in which both her body and her soul are taken up to heaven.[27] This story harks back to traditions about special saints, such as Jeremiah and Enoch, who, in biblical tradition, were also said to be carried up to heaven bodily. When this doctrine appeared in the West in the fifth century it was sufficiently foreign to the tradition to be condemned by the Roman Pope as a heresy.[28]

The doctrinal importance of the establishment of the doctrine of the assumption is considerable. Through a mariological parallel to the ascension (Jesus in the early tradition is also said to have been "taken up" to heaven by God, not to have "risen" through his own power), Mary now becomes available in heaven as an object of prayer and devotion. She is no longer simply a figure of past history. She is established above time in the transcendent realm, where she is present, as is God and the risen Christ, in every time and place. The saints also can come to be seen in this way. But Mary is queen of angels and saints. She is enthroned on the right hand of Christ to reign over the heavenly congregation.

Mary's assumption also means that she is the first of the saints to participate in the resurrection of the body. She anticipates and prefigures the eschatological community of the general resurrection. Again we can see here a reduplication of christological doctrine. In the New Testament, it is the risen Christ who is the "first fruits" of the general resurrection. As Christ comes to be seen primarily as a divinity removed from the human nature of ordinary mortals, the doctrines about him cease to be symbols of the redemption *of humanity*. In effect, the mariological doctrines develop as a recapitulation of the christological ones in order to provide a new figure who represents humanity as such. She stands for the believing community and its anticipation of final redemption, as Christ comes to be seen primarily as the representative of God rather than of humanity.

It is as the representative of the redeemed humanity, purified of sin, the heart of the Church, the queen of the heavenly congregation, and the first fruits of the general resurrection, that Mary becomes that mediatrix of all graces whose star rises in medieval theology, her glory growing ever brighter from the twelfth to the sixteenth centuries, in inverse proportion to the denigration of real women in the flesh. The development of mariological devotion is partly a reaction to the removal of the image of Christ from humanness and the tendency to exalt his image as the stern judge of the final Judgment. Later medieval theology also devoted much attention to the crucified Christ as a figure of agony, but here too he was a terrifying figure as a symbol of unforgivable human guilt.

Mary, then, comes to represent mercy and forgiveness, as Christ comes to be seen primarily as the symbol of guilt and justice. She, like an understanding mother, can make allowances for the inadequacies of sinful humanity. As Christ becomes more fearful, *fiducia* or trust is transferred to Mary. Devotion to her can guarantee that even the worst of sinners has a chance of redemption, for the mother's heart is too tender to allow even the wayward child to be cast off irrevocably (fathers' hearts were clearly not so forgiving). The split between justice and mercy in the images of Christ and Mary also allows some of the stereotypes of female fickleness and partiality to creep into the Mary legends. Mary is seen sometimes as vain and capricious in her favors, protecting those devoted to her in dubious situations, but temperamental to those who neglect her devotion, not unlike her secular counterpart, the Lady of the courtly love tradition.[29] Mary is the beautiful Lady of the heavenly patriarchal court, the tender confidant and merciful mother to whom the trembling sinner could plead his cause against the wrath of the Lord of the castle, sure that her son could not refuse any favor asked him by his mother. She becomes the humanizing element in an otherwise intolerable antithesis of heaven and hell. Mary is the mediatrix of all graces, the center of practical piety, because no one dared hope to find their way into heaven except through her mediation. As it was once said that only through Christ is there a way to the Father, now it is said that only through Mary is there a way to Christ.[30]

The final doctrine of medieval mariological development is the immaculate conception. This doctrine arises as an antechamber to the doctrine of the virgin birth of Christ. Now Mary herself must be cleansed of original sin, so that she can provide the untainted matrix for the birth of the Sinless One. The impulse for the definition of this doctrine derives from Augustine's teaching that original sin is transmitted through the sexual act as inherently sinful, tainting the child that is thereby conceived. The concern to remove Christ from any taint of sinfulness becomes an effort to remove him from any relationship to sinful sexuality. It cannot be that the mother whose womb bore him was herself conceived in sin.

But a formidable impediment lay in the way of such a doctrine. If Mary was born without original sin, she becomes the one exception to the universal sinfulness of mankind and its need for Christ's redemption. Being born without original sin, she would not need Christ's redemption. It was on these grounds that some theologians of the thirteenth century rejected the doctrine of the immaculate conception. Yet Aquinas and others were also sensitive to the problem posed by the birth of the sinless Christ in a womb tainted by original sin; i.e., we see here the tendency to talk of sin as a quasi-material (especially female) "pollution." They compromised by holding that Mary had been conceived in original sin, but cleansed immediately after her conception by a special act of divine grace. The fruits of redemption were applied to her in advance, even in the womb, so that she would provide a sinless womb for the divine maternity.[31] But even this split second of pollution was too much for some thinkers. So, in the fourteenth century, the idea of the immaculate conception gained general acceptance, especially among Franciscan theologians.[32] This cleansing of Mary in the very act of conception could be seen as a special application in advance of the work of Christ, and therefore an inclusion of Mary in the universal forgiveness of sins. But it cannot be believed that she herself ever existed in original sin. Although this doctrine waited for its official definition for the special peculiarities of nineteenth-century ultramontane Catholicism, it had gained general acceptance among theologians in the later Middle Ages. Greek Orthodoxy has not accepted these later mariological views as doctrine, wisely leaving such matters as pious opinion.

The vindication of the doctrine of the immaculate conception in late medieval theology was closely connected with nominalism. Nominalist theology modified the Augustinian tradition of justification. It was said that the human being, by "doing what is in him (her?)" *(facere quod in se est),* can bring the soul to that state of contrition and goodness that corresponded to original created humanity *(natura pura).* This natural conversion is the basis for the penitent's elevation to the state of sanctifying grace and hope for life everlasting won by the cross of Christ. The natural and the supernatural stages of conversion were split from each other and coordinated in a hierarchical manner. The sinner could not win sanctifying grace by natural good works, but the natural will could bring the sinner to that state of repentance which God was bound to reward with the gift of sanctifying grace.

The doctrine of the immaculate conception provided late medieval theology with a symbol for the original or unfallen state of humanity, to which Mary had been restored from the first moment of her existence and which stands for the image of God in every person, that can be restored through repentance and is the ground of the gift of redeeming grace. Mary is the representative of *natura pura*, the capacity of the created nature for perfection.[33] The theological importance of Mariology in Latin theology lies, therefore, not in a covert use of her as a goddess, but precisely in her pure humanity. As representative of humanity in its original goodness, she becomes the anticipation of the eschatological humanity, the concrete realization of the possibility of the final glorification of the human community and the creation in that new heaven and new earth when all reality is reconciled with God. In this sense Mary is the *persona ecclesiae*, the new Israel, the hope of humankind. This is the authentic message of Mariology which is obscured under the false naturalism of nominalism and the antisexuality of the development of the doctrine of the immaculate conception.

The Reformation did not engage in extensive debate about Mariology, but with the Reformation this development was dropped in Protestantism. With the discarding of celibacy, the need for a sublimated feminine figure of monastic psychology evaporated. Since the doctrines of the assumption, the immaculate conception, and even the perpetual virginity of Mary did not appear in Scripture as such, they could not be countenanced by the new biblical exegesis. Protestantism also rejected the nominalist theology with its concept of *natura pura*. It returned to a strict Augustinianism of universal sinfulness and the inability of human nature to win grace by good works. In so doing it tended to regard the original image of God in humanity as totally unavailable. "Human nature" comes to mean only fallen or sinful human nature. Christ alone represents transcendent grace, the dispenser of justifying mercy to a sinful humanity. Mariology, as a symbol of a responding humanity, an original and eschatological possibility of goodness in creation, disappears before an overriding Christology and a primarily negative view of human nature.[34] An exclusively transcendent masculinity alone appears as the symbol of salvation.

But this total disappearance of the feminine symbol from visibility does not mean that Protestantism does not continue to have a doctrine of the "feminine" as the representative of human nature before God. The ecclesiological root of Mariology, as the image of the creaturely self and community in relation to God, continues. Indeed, if anything, Protestantism strengthens the dichotomy between the transcendent masculinity of God, who alone possesses all initiative and power, and the abject passivity of the Christian, represented by the femininity of the Church. The humanizing of Jesus in Pietism transfers this femininity to Jesus, who becomes a mariological figure in relation to the patriarchal Father God. It is Jesus, rather than Mary, who represents humanity in that passive resignation to the will of the Father: ". . . not my will, but thine, be done" (Luke 22:42). Protestant theologians from Luther and Calvin to Karl Barth have found Mariology an acceptable symbol of the Church in this sense of humanity's absolute dependency on God.[35] Thus, in Protestantism more than ever, the super- and sub-ordination between God and creatures, Christ and the Church, is represented by a hierarchical, omnipotent "masculine" God and a passive, self-abnegating "feminine" humanity. The symbolic relations between Christ and the Father, Christ and the Church, and pastor and people continue to enshrine this rigid hierarchical complementarity of male over female.

At this point we must re-evaluate the meaning of Mariology as a liberating symbol for women. Mariology has its appeal for males because it enshrines the dominant ego and active principle as masculine in relation to women, who become the symbol of passive dependency upon the male. Mariology also allows the male to experience this type of "femininity" himself. The most patriarchal theologian can experience himself as passive, receptive, the receptacle of divine grace in relation to God. Receptivity is not a bad thing. Indeed it is a capacity which the mature self must develop. But the patriarchal split between activity and passivity along hierarchical sexist lines destroys authentic receptivity. Receptivity is equated with powerlessness, dependency, and self-hatred, whereas authentic receptivity is only possible from a position of autonomy and self-esteem.

The sexist model of activity and receptivity is sado-masochistic, inculcating domination of subordinates, dependency upon superiors. Males also experience this type of "femininity" in relation to superiors, but one must question whether this constitutes a healthy wholeness. Moreover, the sexist split in the male psyche demands the generic repression of wholeness in women as a group. By equating powerless passivity with "femininity," women are made to be specialists in self-abnegating, auxiliary modes of existence, while males monopolize the effective feedback from *both* forms of experience. Feminists, therefore, must be suspicious of males, especially religious leaders, who too quickly say, "We too need to experience our 'feminine side.' " As long as the "feminine" is equated with the "nature" of women, but the passive, auxiliary "side" of men, this formulation of "androgyny" can only reinforce the traditional model of women as nurturers of a selfhood that can appear only in men.

The liberation of women, as well as men, from sexist hierarchicalism cannot happen as long as this symbolism of masculinity and femininity remains. This symbolism must ever rob women of human integrity, while men, even in their passivity, are given a sado-masochistic model of human relations. The entire psychodynamics of relationships must be entirely transformed, so that activity is not identified with domination, split from a receptivity as dependency. We must envision a new model of reciprocity in which we actualize ourselves by the same processes that we support the autonomy and actualization of others. This demands not only a transvaluation in psychic imagery, but a revolution in power relations between the sexes, representing all power relations of domination and subordination. The symbol for this is not an "androgyny" that still preserves sexist dualism, but that whole personhood in which women can be both I and Thou.

Mariology cannot be a liberating symbol for women as long as it preserves this meaning of "femininity" that is the complementary underside of masculine domination. Mariology becomes a liberating symbol for women only when it is seen as a radical symbol of a new humanity freed from hierarchical power relations, including that of God and humanity. It is here that the revolutionary side of the image of Mary appears, as the representative of the original and eschatological humanity that is repressed from existence within patriarchy, the culture of domination and subjugation. Woman becomes the symbol of the unknown possibility of a humanity beyond and outside the entire system of such a world. Sophia is the matrix and the Ground of Being of the Father God before patriarchy. She is the perfection of humanity beyond the horizon of grace mediated by masculine power symbols of domination. Mary stands for the eschatological humanity of the new covenant: that "new thing" which God has created on earth, "the female overcomes the warrior" (Jer. 31:22). In such a vision the power symbols of God and Christ are meaningful only when they represent the abnegation of domination and the identification with the oppressed.

Mary, in turn, as the *persona* of the new Israel, does not represent the feminine, but that original wholeness of humanity destroyed by sin, for sexism is the original sin of domination that destroys the image of God in humanity and the world. Woman, as the representative of the first and last suppressed person in history, stands for the Church, the new humanity whose nature and possibility remains unrevealed or distorted in a Christianity still modeled on sexist dualisms. She is the reconciled wholeness of women and men, nature and humans, creation and God in the new heaven and the new earth. In her, God already shows mercy and might: the proud are scattered in the imagination of their hearts; the mighty are put down from their thrones, while the humiliated are lifted up; the rich are sent away empty, and the hungry are filled with good things. With such a Mary women might even be able to say: "My soul magnifies the Lord and my spirit rejoices in God my Savior" (Luke 1:46–47). But the Mary whom we should venerate may not be Mother Mary, the woman who represents the patriarchal view that woman's only claim to fame is the capacity to have babies, the relationship which Jesus himself rejected. The Mary who represents the Church, the liberated humanity, may, rather, be the repressed and defamed Mary of the Christian tradition, Mary Magdalene, friend and disciple of Jesus, the first witness of the resurrection, the revealer of the Christian Good News. Blessed is the womb that bore thee, the paps that gave thee suck? Nay, rather, blessed is she who heard the Word of God and kept it (cf. Luke 11:27–28).

Notes

1. Pope Paul VI, "On the Cult of Mary: An Apostolic Exhortation"; Washington, D.C.: United States Catholic Conference, Feb. 2, 1974.
2. Paul Tillich, *Systematic Theology*, III (Chicago: University of Chicago Press, 1963), pp. 293-94.
3. C. G. Jung, *Psychology and Religion* (New Haven, Yale University Press, 1938), p. 77, and *Memories, Dreams and Reflections*, ed. A. Jaffé, trans. R. and C. Winston (New York: Random House, 1961), p. 332.
4. Mary Daly, *Beyond God the Father* (Boston: Beacon Press, 1973), pp. 82-92.
5. See *Religions of the Ancient Near East: Sumero-Akkadian Religious Texts and Ugaritic Epics*, ed. Isaac Mendelsohn (New York: Liberal Arts Press, 1955), pp. 17-46; see also A. S. Kapelrud, *The Violent Goddess: Anath in the Ras Shamra Texts* (Oslo, Universitetsforlaget, 1969); E. O. James, *The Cult of the Mother Goddess* (New York: Praeger, 1959); Erich Neumann, *The Great Mother* (Princeton: Princeton University Press, 1963), esp. chaps. 13-15.
6. Philip Slater, *The Glory of Hera: Greek Mythology and the Greek Family* (Boston: Beacon Press, 1968).
7. Aeschylus, *The Eumenides* 734-46; see also Walter Otto, *The Homeric Gods: The Spiritual Significance of Greek Religion* (London: Thames and Hudson, 1954), chap. 3.
8. Apuleius, *The Golden Ass*, trans. Robert Graves (New York: Pocket Books, 1951), pp. 238-39.
9. *Ibid.,* p. 240.
10. F. F. Hvidberg, *Weeping and Laughter in the Old Testament* (Leiden: Brill, 1962).
11. Raphael Patai, *The Hebrew Goddess* (Ktav, 1967), pp. 45-50.
12. Hosea, chaps. 2,3,9, etc; Jeremiah, chap. 3, etc.
13. *Midrash Rabbah*: Song of Songs, trans. M. Simon (London: Soncino, 1951), p. 18, and *passim.* The saying is ascribed to Rabbi Akiba.

14. Patai, *op. cit.*, pp. 137–56.
15. For the translation and interpretation of Jer. 31:22, see William L. Holladay, "Jeremiah and Women's Liberation," *Andover Newton Quarterly*, 12, no. 4 (March 1972), pp. 213–22.
16. Sergius Bulgakov, *The Orthodox Church* (London: Centenary Press, 1935), pp. 139ff.; see also Bulgakov, *The Wisdom of God* (London: Williams and Northgate, 1937).
17. H. H. Rowley, "The Interpretation of the Song of Songs," *Journal of Theological Studies*, 38 (1937): 337–63.
18. John of the Cross, *The Spiritual Canticle*, and *The Living Flame of Love*; Teresa of Ávila, *The Interior Castle*.
19. Mark 6:3; Matt. 13:55; Luke 4:22; Mark 3:31–35; Matt. 12:46–50; see also John 7:3; Acts 1:13–14; I Cor. 15:5–7; Gal. 1:19; 2:9, 12; Acts 15:13; I Cor. 9:5; cf. Tertullian, *De Monogamia* 8; *De Carne Christe* 7; *Ad Marcion* 19; see also Hegesippus, in R. M. Grant, *Second Century Christianity; A Collection of Fragments* (London, 1946), pp. 57ff. An earlier tradition than the infancy narratives, still preserved in the New Testament, assumed Jesus to be the natural son of Joseph; see R. Ruether, "The Brothers of Jesus and the Virginity of Mary," *Continuum* (Spring 1969), pp. 93–105.
20. Mary Magdalene is a central figure in Gnostic Gospels: "The Lord loved Mary more than all the disciples and kissed her on the mouth often": Gospel of Philip, III: 35; see also Gospel of Thomas 114 and Gospel of Mary 17–18.
21. Justin Martyr, *Dialogue with Trypho* 100, 3; Irenaeus, *Adversus Haereses* V, 19, 1; H. Koch, *Virgo Eva-Virgo Maria* (Berlin, 1937).
22. The idea of the perpetual virginity of Mary appears first in *Proevangelium of James*, whose traditions go back to *ca.* A.D. 200. See H. Campenhausen, *The Virgin Birth in the Theology of the Ancient Church* (Naperville, Ill.: Allenson, 1964).
23. Jerome, *Against Helvidius on the Perpetual Virginity of Mary*, Library of the Nicene and Post-Nicene Fathers, 2nd. ser., vol. 6, pp. 334–45; see also Ep. 48, to Pammachius.
24. Athanasius, *Orationes contra Arianos* III, 14, 29; see also G. Miegge, *The Virgin Mary* (London: Lutterworth, 1955), pp. 53–67.
25. *Ibid.*, pp. 75–76.
26. Pseudo John the Evangelist, *The Book of the Falling*

Asleep of the Holy Mother of God, Ante-Nicene Fathers, VIII: 587–91.

27. Pseudo Melito, *Transitus Mariae: Apocryphal New Testament* (1924); see R. L. P. Milburn, *Early Christian Interpretations of History,* appendix: "The Assumption of Mary" (New York: Harper & Row, 1954); also W. Burghardt, *The Testimony of the Patristic Age of Mary's Death* (Westminster, Md.: Newman, 1957).

28. Meigge, *op. cit.,* p. 86 (Pope Gelasius, A.D. 492–96).

29. Eleanor McLaughlin, "Equality of Souls, Inequality of Sexes: Women in Medieval Theology," *Religion and Sexism,* ed. R. Ruether (New York: Simon and Schuster, 1974), pp. 249–51.

30. The classic text of Marian devotion is St. Alfonso de' Liguori, *The Glories of the Most Holy Mary* (1750); see Miegge, *op. cit.,* pp. 141–44; see also J. B. Carol, *Mariology,* vol. 2 (Milwaukee: Bruce Publishing Co., 1955), pp. 377–460.

31. Aquinas, *Sum. Theo.,* III, Q. 27, Art. 1–6; G. Miegge, *op. cit.,* pp. 116–17; see also J. B. Carol, *Mariology,* vol. 1, pp. 300–1, 366.

32. Miegge, *op. cit.,* pp. 123–26; J. B. Carol, *op. cit.,* vol. 1, pp. 302–8, 366–69.

33. Heiko Obermann, *The Harvest of Medieval Theology* (Cambridge, Mass.: Harvard University Press, 1963), pp. 281–322.

34. Heiko Obermann, *Mary in Evangelical Perspective* (Philadelphia: Fortress, 1971).

35. Thomas O'Meara, *Mary in Protestant and Catholic Theology* (New York: Sheed and Ward, 1966), pp. 111–45; Karl Barth, *Church Dogmatics,* I/2, pp. 139–52.

Guarding the Sanctuary:
Sexism and Ministry

THE EXCLUSION OF WOMEN FROM THE CHRISTIAN MINISTRY can be studied on two levels. First, one can trace historic developments in the New Testament which presaged a greater participation of women in the leadership of the Church, and then their gradual exclusion from leadership with its accompanying rationalizations. Second, one can examine the symbolic structures in theology which make it difficult for women to be seen as representing the "leadership principle."

In an article a few years ago Leonard Swidler announced that "Jesus Was a Feminist." [1] Some feminist thinkers have chosen to brush this idea aside, declaring that "even if Jesus wasn't a feminist, I am." [2] However, the importance of a more just appraisal of the view of women in the Gospels is not simply a matter of winning Jesus' blessing upon the feminist movement although, culturally speaking, that is hardly an unimportant issue. It is also a question of recovering another dimension of women's history which has been repressed. If one could not find in the historical traditions moments when the truth was glimpsed, surely we would begin to wonder about all our capacities for humanity.

WOMEN IN THE NEW TESTAMENT

A reading of the synoptic Gospels reveals a startling element of iconoclasm toward the traditional subordination of women in Jewish life. This contrast between the feminism of Jesus and traditional Judaism should not, of course, be used to buttress a new Christian anti-

Judaism. Patriarchy is not peculiarly Jewish, and Jesus was interpreting his critical views in the light of the prophetic and eschatological horizon of Jewish faith itself. I will mention a few of the more obvious expressions of this feminism of Jesus and early Christian life.

Jesus had close women friends and disciples, and they are pictured as accompanying him on his preaching and teaching trips, and as remaining faithful to him to the end, even when the other disciples had all deserted him. Mary Magdalene (who is nowhere in the New Testament identified as a former "sinner"),[3] Joanna, and Susanna are named as among Jesus' followers who accompany him and the twelve on journeys, in a way that must have seemed highly unconventional in traditional society (Luke 8:1-3). Jesus often contrasts the faithlessness of the social and religious establishment with the faith of poor widows and outcast women (Luke 21:1-4; 7:36-50). Jesus does his first miracles for women (Matt. 8:14ff.; Mark 1:30-31; Luke 4:38-39; John 2:1-11); and, at the critical moment of his disappointment in Jerusalem, he describes himself as feeling like a "mother hen" (Matt. 23:37; Luke 13:34). Jewish law regarded a woman with a flow of blood as unclean and polluting anyone whom she touched. Jesus' reaction to the woman with a hemorrhage shows his deliberate discarding of this taboo, while the woman's own terror at being discovered in touching his garment reveals her awareness of having violated this taboo (Mark 5:25-34; Matt. 9:20-22; Luke 8:43-48).

Jesus also violates the law which forbids the Jewish male to speak alone with any woman not his wife, let alone a Samaritan, as is shown by the astonishment of the disciples (John 4:27). Even Jesus' pronouncements on divorce must be seen in the context of a society where a woman, who had no means of support, could be cast out by her husband on the slightest pretext. The stricter attitude toward divorce in Jesus' time had the purpose of providing women with greater respect and security in marriage (Matt. 19:3–9; Mark 10:2–10; Luke 16:18). It is Jesus' women friends who remain faithful to him through the crucifixion and burial. They, especially his closest friend Mary Magdalene, are the first witnesses of the resurrection. Jewish law also regarded women as incapable of acting as responsible witnesses. To make women the first witnesses of the resurrection was to make them the original source of the credibility of the Christian faith (Matt. 28:1; Mark 16:1; Luke 24:10, 22–25; John 20:1ff.).

But perhaps even more important than this element of relationship to women in Jesus' life is Jesus' modeling of the Christian ministry on the role of service. The waiting on tables, the lowly role of women and servants, is to be the model for the ministry. When the sons of Zebedee ask if they can sit on the right and left hand of Jesus at the judgment, Jesus calls them to him and says:

> You know that the rulers of the Gentiles lord it over them, and their great men exercise authority over them. It shall not be so among you; but whoever would be great among you must be your servant, and whoever would be first among you must be your slave, even as the Son of man came not to be served but to serve. (Matthew 20:25–28)

Traditional theological images of God as father have been the sanctification of sexism and hierarchicalism precisely by defining this relationship of God as father to humanity in a domination-subordination model and by allowing ruling-class males to identify themselves with this divine fatherhood in such a way as to establish themselves in the same kind of hierarchical relationship to women and lower classes. Jesus, however, refers to God as father in such a way as to overthrow this hierarchical relationship of the rulers over the ruled. No Christian leadership group is to arise which is to associate itself with divine titles of leadership or fatherhood in such a way as to establish itself in a hierarchical relationship to other Christians.

> But you are not to be called rabbi, for you have one teacher, and you are all brothers [and sisters]. And call no man father on earth, for you have one Father, who is in heaven. Neither be called masters, for you have one master, the Christ. He who is greatest among you shall be your servant. (Matthew 23:8–11)

If this teaching of Jesus had been maintained, the very root of sexism and clericalist hierarchicalism in biblical religion would have been decisively undercut. The fatherhood of God could not have been understood as establishing male ruling-class power over subjugated groups in the Church or Christian society, but as that equal fatherhood that makes all Christians equals, brothers and sisters.

Yet although Jesus held up the image of service to overthrow a ruling-class concept of hierarchical power for men, he does not use this image of service to reinforce the image of women as servants. On the contrary, the one person whom he rebukes for being "much occupied with serving" is a woman, Martha. In traditional Judaism the place of women was in the kitchen. Men alone were called to study the Torah with the rabbi. By vindicating Mary's right to join the circle of disciples and students of the Teacher, Jesus overthrows the traditional concept of women's place as upheld by Martha. "Mary has chosen the better part which shall not be taken from her" (Luke 10:38–42). The principles of Christian community are founded upon a role transformation between men and women, rulers and ruled. The ministry of the Church is not to be modeled on hierarchies of lordship, but on the *diakonia* of women and servants, while women are freed from exclusive identification with the service role and called to join the circle of disciples as equal members.

These views of women had their effect on the earliest Christian community. The parallelism of male and female examples in the parables shows that women were included equally with men as students of the Christian catechesis—which would not have been the case in the synagogue.[4] The Pauline letters also show that women were prominent among early Christian leaders, both in local churches and among traveling evangelists. In Philippians Paul addresses a person whom he calls "true yokefellow" and whom he asks to reconcile two women, Euodia and Syntyche. These two women, Paul says, labored side by side with him and Barnabas in the proclamation of the gospel (4:2–3). As known and addressed as church leaders, Prisc(ill)a is generally named first of this husband-and-wife team who headed the church at Corinth and later went to Ephesus (Acts 18:18, 26; Rom. 16:3; 2 Tm. 4:19). Many other women are mentioned in the salutations of Paul to the leaders of local churches (Rom. 16). Women evidently moved great distances between churches as Christian evangelists, as is evidenced by the recommendation of the deaconess Phoebe from the church at Cenchrea to the church at Rome (or Ephesus?) (Rom. 16:1).

Would Paul have regarded any of these women as ordained to the priesthood or the episcopacy? Paul does not use these titles of leadership in his authentic epistles, relegating the office of overseer to a minor managerial function (I Cor. 12:28). Paul's concept of ministry is charismatic, established by the actual gifts and functions which a person exercises in the community. These women mentioned by Paul clearly exercise the functions which he describes as those of apostles (traveling evangelists), prophets, and teachers. Even the famous passage in I Corinthians 11, where Paul declares that women should cover their heads, indicates that Paul did assume, in fact, that women were vocal in the congregation as leaders of prayer and prophecy.

Paul, however, was a theological radical, but, at least provisionally, a social conservative. In Christ "there is neither Jew nor Greek, there is neither slave nor free,

there is neither male nor female" (Gal. 3:28). The redemption won by Christ has abolished the distinction between races, classes, and sexes in the eyes of God and
in the Christian congregation. But he was unwilling to
allow this breakthrough in the Christian community to
create revolutionary changes in social roles in ordinary
society. This social conservativism can be seen in his attitudes both toward women and toward slaves (Col.
3:18–4:1). In regard to these social roles Paul follows a
conventional theology that sees the hierarchicalism between slaves and masters, women and men, as established by the orders of creation. Paul does not know the
teachings of Jesus that forbade men to associate themselves with God the Father or with Christ to establish a
hierarchical relationship over other persons. Instead, the
relationship of God or Christ to the Church is seen as a
model of the relationship of male to female (I Cor. 11:3;
and, if authentically Pauline, Eph. 5:22–24). Women are
also made the source of sin, according to the Genesis
story that made the origin of demons in the world the
fault of women. Women are admonished to cover their
heads as a sign of their subjugation because of this sin (I
Cor. 11:4–10).[5] Thus when Paul talks about the orders of
creation, he remains a patriarchal conservative. When he
talks about redemption in Christ, he becomes a radical.
Yet it is important to realize that he himself did not expect these orders of creation to last and even speaks of
them as demonic. His admonition that all—women,
slaves, subjects—should stay in their places, and not
use equality in Christ to seek social change, is in the
context of an expectation that very soon Christ would return and these powers and principalities of the cosmos
would disappear (Rom. 13:11).

   But these statements of Paul, reinforcing the present
orders of creation, when taken out of their context in
Paul's imminent eschatological expectation, become
conservative statements which absolutize the status quo

of a sexist, class, and slave society. These statements of Paul are still being used today to reinforce the subjugation of women and were used by American theologians until the Emancipation Proclamation to justify slavery.[6] The very heart of the gospel was discarded to re-establish domination-subjugation relationships between Christians in the Church and in Christian societies. To understand Paul's theology correctly we must interpret the relationship of the eschatological breakthrough in Jesus, which abolished sex, class, and racist subjugation, not as a spiritual principle unconnected with social reality, but as a principle that must leaven social reality to create a just society where all peoples are seen as sisters, brothers, and friends, rather than as masters and servants.

In the later strata of the New Testament we can see this movement back to traditional patriarchal relations of men and women in the Church. The deutero-Pauline pastoral epistles move from Paul's charismatic concept of ministry to a patriarchal ministry modeled after the synagogue and the traditional family. Married men, who have shown themselves to be firm husbands and fathers, are to be the bishops and elders. Women, on the other hand, are told to

> learn in silence with all submissiveness. I permit no woman to teach or to have authority over men; she is to keep silent. (I Timothy 2:11–12)

Her secondary place in the order of creation and her primary responsibility for the fall are cited as the theological basis of this subordination (I Tim. 2:13–14). Yet the very vehemence of this statement suggests that the author is trying to negate an established tradition in many churches where women were given the right to teach and to lead.

This deutero-Pauline development seems to be responsible for the passage which appears in Paul's first letter to the Corinthians (14:34); which has been the passage most frequently cited to prohibit, not only ministry for women in the Church, but even the right of women to speak in public in society:

> . . . the women should keep silence in the churches. For they are not permitted to speak, but should be subordinate, as even the law says.

Robin Scroggs and other New Testament exegetes have judged this passage to be an interpolation.[7] The passage interrupts the surrounding line of thought. When this passage is removed, the following sentence, "What! Did the word of God originate with you . . . ?" Makes sense as a reference to the previous discussion of prophecy. Both the legalism of the language and its inconsistency with Paul's actual practice, as evidenced only three chapters earlier, betray its post-Pauline derivation. Probably the passage was interpolated into the authentic epistles of Paul from the pastorals when the Pauline collection was edited a generation after Paul's death. Yet even this patriarchal Church of the pastorals continued to ordain women deacons (I Tim. 3:11).

THE MINISTRY OF WOMEN IN CHURCH HISTORY

The abolition of deaconesses took place gradually between the second and sixth centuries. There is evidence that some churches also ordained women *presbyterae* or priests during these centuries.[8] But the decisive blow to the ordination of women came with the triumph of a sacerdotal-caste concept of the priesthood in the fourth century. When Constantine made the Christian Church the official religion of the empire, the Christian ministry was established as a social caste and received the privileges traditionally reserved for the pagan priesthood of the official cultus, such as exemption from property taxes and military service. A cultic concept of worship shaped the ministry and liturgy into a new temple cultus. As a result the Old Testament laws of cultic purity were revived and applied to the Christian priests, defining women as unclean and to be strictly excluded from the sanctuary. Canon laws of this time show that the uncleanness of women was used as a chief reason for eliminating the office of deaconess. Even lay women were advised to stay away from communion during menstruation.[9]

The growing asceticism of the Church compounded these earlier sources of misogynism. Women were seen as the symbol of dangerous carnality. They should be segregated in church, veiled; they must not speak or learn except in the privacy of the cloister. The priesthood, in turn, was molded into a cultic caste, whose sacral purity is maintained by strict segregation from all that is female. The irrationality of some of the recent reactions to the ordination of women to the priesthood in the Episcopal Church reflects the unconscious persistence of this concept of a male sacral purity which is created by rigid demarcation of the sanctuary against the "pollution" of the female. This concept of women as both unclean and sexually threatening is reflected in Catholic canon law, where the laws referring to women have to do primarily with excluding them from the sanctuary and from personal contact with priests.[10]

However, the maleness of Jesus was not used in patristic theology as an argument against the ordination of women. Indeed the Church Fathers maintained that "that which is not incarnated is not redeemed." This implies that the incarnation of Christ redeems generic human nature, and not male sexual particularity.[11] Otherwise women could not be baptized either. The mystical tradition follows Paul's concept that in Christ the demarcation between male and female is overcome and speaks of Christ as androgynous.[12]

However, medieval scholastic theology adopted the Aristotelian anthropology which defined women as "misbegotten males." As noted earlier, Thomas Aquinas followed Aristotle in believing that the male semen provides the entire genetic formation of the embryo. The mother furnishes only the "blood" or material substance that builds up the body. Normatively, every male seed would produce another male. Women are born when the lower material principle gains an aberrant dominance over the higher formative principle, producing a "misbegotten male" or female. Women are seen as biologically defective, both physically and in their capacity for thought and moral self-discipline. They are inherently servile, being to the male as the body is to its head. On these grounds Thomas regarded women as inferior by nature and more prone to sin in the disorder of the fall. The incarnation can take place only in a male who represents full humanity and contains the full image of God, while Thomas, following Augustine,[13] declares that women by themselves do not possess the image of God, but only when taken together with the male who is their "head." Women, therefore, cannot exercise "headship" in the Church or in society. Hence only males can be priests and represent Christ.[14]

The logic of this Thomistic position finds its extreme expression in the *Malleus Maleficarum*, the handbook on the persecution of witches written by two Dominican inquisitors in the fifteenth century. Women are defined as inherently defective and perverse and doubly prone to the demonic after the fall. The maleness of Jesus, however, is said to have preserved males from so great an evil as witchcraft. The very word used for witches is female, and the inquisitors define witches as normatively female.[15] Here Thomas's androcentric theology comes close to excluding women from essential humanity and the fruits of redemption. Indeed every attempt to justify the exclusion of women from ordination on the grounds of some difference in nature results logically in an impugning of their essential humanity and capacity for baptism as well.

The Reformation did not immediately change this historic exclusion of women from the ministry, since they took St. Paul's dictum that women should keep silent as normative. However, they rejected celibacy as a superior path of virtue and rehabilitated the family as the basic model of the Church. They also sought to create an educated laity, which included women. The Calvinist sense of personal conscience was potentially revolutionary for women, as well as other subjugated groups, although this was counteracted by a patriarchal concept of the father as minister of the family, as the preacher was the father of the congregation. The Calvinist ministry would be more likely to uphold a woman's right of conscience if she were opposing a Catholic or an Anglican father or husband than if she were criticizing themselves. Yet Calvinism soon produced its share of independent women, such as Anne Hutchinson in Massachusetts, who took these Protestant principles to apply to themselves.

The inclusion of women in the ordained ministry of Protestant churches is based on two developments in modern times. The first is a more critical historical exegesis of the Scripture, which allows the antifemale passages in Paul and the pastorals to be put aside for more fundamental theological principles. The second is the impetus provided by liberalism in society with its vindication of the rights of women to equality in civil rights, education, and the professions. Today it is primarily traditionalist churches with a cultic concept of the priesthood and biblical fundamentalist churches which still refuse to ordain women. Yet even the Protestant churches which have adopted a liberal view still preserve a symbolic structure in their ecclesiological language which makes it hard to install women visibly as the leading pastor of a congregation. Today only about 2 percent of the ministry of these churches are women, and most of these have been hidden along the side lines of the ministry, such as directors of religious education.[16] To understand this problem it is necessary to examine these symbolic structures, to see how the language of ecclesiology preserves the sexist world-view.

SEXISM, CLERICALISM, AND ECCLESIOLOGY

Sexism is based symbolically on misappropriated dualisms. The dialectics of human existence: mind/body, spirituality/carnality, being/becoming, truth/appearance, life/death—these dualisms are identified as male and female and are socially projected upon men and women as their "natures." The meaning of the feminine thus becomes modeled in classical spirituality on the images of the lower self and world. Autonomous spiritual selfhood is imaged (by males, the cultural creators of this view) as intrinsically masculine, while the feminine becomes the symbol of the repressed, subjugated and dreaded "abysmal" side of "man."

I have already shown that the ultimate theological rationale for the hierarchical symbolism of masculinity and femininity is the image of God as transcendent Father. Creation becomes the wife or bride of the "sky Father." Most images of God in religions are modeled after the ruling class of society. In biblical religion the image of God is that of a patriarchal Father above the visible created world, who relates to Israel as his "wife" and "children" in the sense of creatures totally dependent on his will, owing him unquestioning obedience. This image allows the king and patriarchal class to relate to their women, children, and servants through the same model of domination and dependency. The relation of God to Israel and Christ to the Church becomes modeled after the patriarchal marriage relationship. I have suggested that Jesus was trying to reinterpret the image of the fatherhood of God, so that it could no longer be used to establish a ruling class of "fathers" who related to dependent people through the model of a hierarchical relation of God to his creatures. But this imagery finds its way back

into Christian theology in Paul, who models the relationship of husband to wife after that of the divine Lord to
creation or the Church.[17] Thus the Church comes to be
imaged as a bride or mother in relation to the divine fatherhood of God.

The femininity of the Church does not mean that its
leaders can be women, of course! That is to say, the
church leadership does not see itself as representing the
Church before God (Mary), but as representing God before the Church. Contrary to Jesus' teaching, a leadership class rises in the Church that models itself after
divine patriarchy in order to establish itself in a hierarchical relation to the Christian people. It is not clear that this
development has taken place in the New Testament,
even though the symbolism for it is established in Paul.
But there is no leadership caste called fathers or priests
in the New Testament. Indeed, the Epistle to the Hebrews
explicitly forbids the creation of a new priesthood "who
are many in number," since Christ alone is High Priest,
and all Christians are called to be a "priestly people."
But this hierarchical concept of leadership is evident in
the letters of Ignatius of Antioch in the early second century, who compares the bishop to God the Father in relationship to the people.[18]

This image of leadership splits the Church into two
groups, a clerical caste who represent the transcendent
"male" principle hierarchically related to a "female" or
"passive" principle. Both clericalism and the pacification
of the laity operate out of this symbolic psychology. The
clergy are seen as bringing all grace and truth from
"above." The people cease to be seen as possessing
self-generating capacities for leadership by which they
can bless, teach, forgive, or ordain one another. Instead
they must receive the "seminal word" or "grace" as a
power above and beyond themselves, which the clergy
alone possess and mediate to them. The people assume
the prone, passive position before the raised altars and

pulpits of the "fathers." The laity becomes "women-children" symbolically, and often actually as well, while the self-imagery of the clergy excludes the possibility of women exercising the hierarchical functions.

However, if we are to understand the modern identity crisis of the clergy and the particular vehemence with which women ministers are resisted, even in liberal churches, we have to analyze the way this "feminine" or passive image of the Church has been reshaped by the changed relationship of Church and state in secularized society. In the nineteenth century the Church lost its established relation to public political power, which it had had since Constantine, and was domesticated in the private sector of life. A dramatic shift in the imagery of the feminine also takes place in the nineteenth century with romanticism, which reflects a reaction to the new industrial, secular work-world and a location of the religious values in private life. The home, as the institution of "private man," becomes the repository of a nostalgic religiosity. Thus, as we have seen, public society loses any official relation to God or the sacred and becomes the realm of materialism, power, and functional rationality. The traditional split between Church and world now becomes a split between the home and the world, with "Christian man" located in the home or the private, domestic sector.

However, since the home is the sphere of women, "Christian man" comes to mean primarily "woman." The domestication of the Church furthers an identification of women with spirituality, morality, and piety, over against the secular masculine sphere of materialism, work, and scientific rationality. A reshaping of the dominant image of the feminine takes place. Whereas in classical Christianity, women had represented the "carnal" over against a male spirituality and rationality, now women come to be seen as more religious, spiritual, and moral than men—though, of course, this does not alter the image of them as irrational. But rationality loses its connections with "wisdom," or moral and spiritual values, and comes to be identified with the technological rationality of science. Rationality is directed toward manipulating the material world of work, rather than the elevation of the spirit. Morality and religion are divorced from reason and identified with a sentimentalized concept of the "feminine." The changing image of Jesus from the kingly Pantocrator of the Byzantine tradition to the sweet girllike figure of nineteenth-century pietism seems to reflect this change also.

Secularization means that the Church, too, finds itself structured, psychically and socially, in the domestic sphere. The clergy become "out of place" in the world of "real men," the world of power and business. They now serve primarily to pacify the powerless—women, children, private citizens—in relation to the male power structures of secular society. Males in the work-world value the Church in this role of domestic pacifier, but also accord the clergy that underhanded contempt with which the masculinist ethic always regards the feminine, that is, that which it has pacified and domesticated in relation to itself. Such men are embarrassed or angered by clergy who "don't know their place" and who try to interfere in things that they "know nothing about," such as political and economic power. Thus the clergy, who have inherited classical masculinist self-images in relation to women and the congregation, now find themselves serving essentially the feminine role in relation to the real power structures of society.

Many who become clergy under these circumstances tend to be men with insecure egos who feel the need of an office which automatically establishes their superiority, without having to be really challenged by other people, especially females, as equals. The mere possibility that women might breach this bastion of male privilege induces panic, as though the appearance of women in the priestly role will automatically reveal the males there as dressed in skirts. Others declare that men in the Church will flee, leaving the place entirely to women. Some of the strange statements that have come from those resisting the ordination of women in the Episcopal Church, such as the pronouncement that to "ordain women would be spiritual lesbianism," [19] reveal the sexual role conflicts of the present situation of the clergy.

THE LIBERATION OF WOMEN AND THE CHURCH

The symbolic imagery of masculinity and femininity in the relation of clergy and laity, clergy and secular society, has reached a contradictory impasse which makes the clergy either the final embattled bastion of insecure male ego or else the place where the psycho-symbolic dynamics of this entire tradition must be rethought. The question of women leadership in the Church is certainly a question of the human rights of women, the vindication of the full humanity of women in the Church. It is sometimes said that no one has a right to be ordained, and therefore one cannot speak of ordaining women as a question of rights.[20] But this argument misconstrues the issue. It is not a question of any individual having a right to be ordained as an individual. It is a matter of an entire group of Christians, over half the membership of the Church, being excluded from the possibility of ordination on the basis of group characteristics, such as sex or race. If Negroes were excluded from ordination on grounds of race, we would well recognize that such a practice uses the ministry of the Church to establish the principle of their human inferiority. It is clear that this exclusion of women from ordination has been established in the Church precisely on the basis of false anthropologies which regard women as inferior human beings.

But the ordination of women also threatens the entire psychodynamics by which the God-human, the soul-body, the clergy-lay, and finally the Church-world relationships have been imaged in terms of sexual hierarchicalism. It is not enough, therefore, just to insert one or two female persons, oddly, into the present shape of the ministry, and then assume that all the other symbolic structures can go on as before. The entrance of women into the ministry regularly (rather than just exceptionally, as is the case with those churches which ordain women), must throw into question all the relationships which have been modeled on sexual hierarchicalism. A psychological revolution would be required in the way we relate to God, to leadership, to each other, to "the world," and to nature. The conservatives are correct in recognizing that the revolution represented by the ordination of women threatens the foundations of the whole symbolic structure, and one must understand the antipathy to it as much deeper than the flimsy reasoning of the arguments which they usually give against it.

But these reasons for the profoundly threatening character of women's ordination are also the reasons why one must regard it as necessary, in order to rediscover the meaning of the gospel. These dualisms, symbolized by sexism, incarnate a heritage of self-alienation and social projection of inferior and auxiliary humanity onto women. Racism, the subjugation of lower classes and colonized peoples, and even anti-Semitism operate out of much the same language of sexist dualism, i.e., the elevation of the "head" people over the "body" people. This same psychology also blinds us to our ravaging of nature and the amorality of technology. The Church has allowed itself to become the cultural guardian of these symbols of domination and subjugation. This role is an apostasy to the mission of the Church as the representative of liberated humanity. Instead the Church becomes the sacralizer and last stronghold of the "old order," presiding over the final sanctuary where these alienations are perpetuated.

Women who are ordained cannot be content to assimilate themselves into the clericalist mentality, although many women are perfectly capable of doing so. They must recognize that women's ordination is the first part of the larger challenge to the clericalist relation of ministry and people. Clericalism is sexism raised to the second power. Since the clergy-lay relationship has been modeled after sexist hierarchicalism, women in the ministry must find it fundamentally incongruous to continue this psychology of clergy-lay relationships.

Leadership must change from the princely and paternalistic modes to a dialogical relationship, where ministry is seen primarily as the skill to evoke the gifts and creative initiatives of the whole community. It is the people, not the "ministers," who are finally the agents of the ministry and mission of the Church. The Word is not seen as a fiat which comes from the raised pulpit, from above and beyond the people, reducing the people to passive "feminine" or "infantile" receivers. Rather, it springs into being in the midst of the community in dialogue. Sacramental grace is not a private possession of a sacerdotal caste, but the foundation of the life of the community. Its liturgy and organs of ministry are its own self-articulation of the life in the Holy Spirit upon which the community is founded. The Church, as a community, is called to teach one another, support one another, forgive one another, celebrate together, and engage in theological self-reflection upon its own life together.

This community-centered view of ministry must also alter our model of the relationship of God to creation and the Church. God is not seen as the domineering Father who reduces "his creation" to the prone position before his activity and might, but rather as the Holy Spirit who is the Ground of Being of creation and the new creation. The Church rises, as the community of the new creation, out of the activity of the Holy Spirit which renews the world. This work of the Spirit does not found a hierarchy through whom God's power trickles down until it finally reaches the lowest level in the local community. Rather, the foundation of the local community is primary. Ministry is simply the self-articulation of the community's life together. By designating certain people to exercise these functions, the people do not lose these powers, but simply order and express the life which is theirs. Ministry and community must be seen in a reciprocal relationship. The designation of leaders is in order to activate and develop the ministry of the community, rather than to pacify it in relation to themselves.

I think this understanding of ministry, community, and its foundation in grace must also change our model of the processes of education and ordination of ministry. At best, the processes of selecting and educating an ordained ministry should arise from within the self-educative process of the community itself. With trained and committed teachers, the community should be engaged, first of all, in theological self-reflection on its own mission. Out of this process especially talented and committed persons develop who are designated by the congregation for more specialized training, to be equipped to become teachers and pastors. Ministerial education should be based on the education of the adult community. For more specialized training in theological and social skills, congregations might band together to create schools. The designating of a person as an ordained leader of a congregation should then be carried out in such a way as to show that it is the community itself which ordains her or him.

However, at the present time seminary education is designed to maximize the schism between clergy and laity. Seminary training has no organic connection with a group of communities. The content becomes a critical, esoteric "archeology" which has almost lost any relationship to the hermeneutics of prophetic preaching and pastoring of the Church. The people, in turn, remain in a precritical religious culture, and are left ignorant of the developments of critical theological education. As a result a trauma takes place when the conventionally religious lay person goes to college. When the liberally trained minister comes to the congregation, "he" finds a cultural impasse which is almost unbridgeable, and generally "he" either leaves out of frustration or else accommodates "himself" to a style of religiosity which contradicts "his" education. The gap between clerical and lay education thus reinforces the paternalistic relationship of clergy to the laity and an infantile culture in the Church. This situation cannot be changed by ad hoc measures. It demands turning the entire system around. The best theological education should be located in the self-education of the local community. The community itself should arise through a process by which it itself shapes a common faith and commitment. Only then can we even begin to speak meaningfully about ministry, community, and mission.

But this overcoming of self-alienation within the life of the Church—between male and female, clergy and people, theological education and ministry—can happen only as a part of the overcoming of the most fundamental alienation of all, the alienation between the "real world" and the encapsulation of the Church in the sphere of privatized sentimentality. If both the clergy and women must see themselves as victims of this encapsulation in the domestic sphere, then they must also recognize each other as common allies in a struggle to overthrow the false schism between "private morality" and the world of "real men." In order even to begin to pray again Jesus' prayer that God's "will be done on earth, as it is in heaven," we must dissolve the false dichotomy between a pacified morality and the public world of technological rationality which renders the message of the Church "effete" while the masters of war go about their "manly" activities. The gospel of the Church must again come to be recognized as the social mandate of human history, not the means of setting up a new regime of domination or, on the other hand, of withdrawing into a private world of individual "salvation."

The liberation of all human relations from the false polarities of masculinity and femininity must also shape a new relationship of humanity to nature. The project of human life must cease to be seen as one of "domination of nature," or exploitation of a bodily reality which is outside and other than ourselves. Rather, we have to find a new language of ecological responsiveness, a reciprocity between consciousness and the world systems in which we live and move and have our being. Our final mandate is to redeem our sister, the earth, from her bondage to destruction, recognizing her as our partner in the creation of that new world where all things can be "very good." Thus the exorcism of the demonic spirit of sexism in the Church touches off a revolution which must transform all the relations of alienation and domination— between self and body, between leaders and community, between person and person, between social groups, between Church and world, between humanity and nature, finally our model of God in relation to creation—all of which have been modeled on the sexist schizophrenia. Sexism reflects both the heart and the ultimate circumference of the many revolutions in which we are presently involved.

Notes

1. Leonard Swidler, "Jesus Was a Feminist," *Catholic World*, January 1971.

2. Mary Daly, *Beyond God the Father* (Boston: Beacon Press, 1973), p. 73.

3. The statement in Luke 8:2–3 that Jesus drove devils from Mary Magdalene and the other women with him refers to physical infirmities not to sin. In a post-New Testament development Mary Magdalene came to be identified in popular imagination with the woman who anointed Jesus (a sinner according to Luke 7:36–50, but not according to Mark 14:3–9/Matt. 26:6–13/John 12:1–8).

4. Matt. 24:40–41; 25:1–30; Luke 13:18–21; 15:3–8; see also Constance Parvey, "The Theology and Leadership of Women in the New Testament," *Religion and Sexism: Images of Women in the Jewish and Christian Traditions*, ed. Rosemary Ruether (New York: Simon and Schuster, 1974), pp. 139ff.

5. Gen. 6:2–4; cf. Bernard P. Prusak, "Woman: Seductive Siren and Source of Sin?" *Religion and Sexism*, pp. 89–116.

6. George D. Armstrong, *The Christian Doctrine of Slavery* (New York: Scribner's, 1857); based on the epistles of Paul.

7. Robin Scroggs, "Paul and Eschatological Woman," *Journal of the American Academy of Religion*, XL, no. 3 (September 1972), pp. 283–303.

8. Clara Maria Henning, "Canon Law and the Battle of the Sexes," *Religion and Sexism*, pp. 275–79.

9. *Ibid.*, p. 273.

10. *Ibid.*, pp. 269–73.

11. Gregory of Nazianzus, Ep. 101, to Cledonius (on Apollinarianism): Migne, *P.G.*, vol. 37, 181C.

12. The Rabbis regarded Adam as originally androgynous; see Louis Ginzberg, *The Legends of the Jews* (Philadelphia: Jewish Publication Society, 1955), vol. 5 (notes to vols. 1 and 2), n. 42, pp. 88–89. The Gnostics believed that this an-

drogyny was restored by Christ; see R. M. Grant, *The Secret Sayings of Jesus* (Garden City, N.Y.: Doubleday, 1960), pp. 143ff.: This view continued in Christian mysticism. For a modern statement of it, see Georg Koepgen, *Die Gnosis des Christentums* (Salzburg, 1939), pp. 315ff.; cf. C. G. Jung, *Mysterium Coniunctionis* (New York: Pantheon, 1963), pp. 373–74.

13. Augustine, *De Trinitate* 7, 7, 10.

14. Eleanor McLaughlin, "Equality of Souls, Inequality of Sexes: Women in Medieval Theology," *Religion and Sexism*, pp. 215–20.

15. *Malleus Maleficarum*, Heinrich Krämer and Jacob Sprenger (1486), trans. Montague Summers (London, J. Rodker, 1928), pt. I, sec. 6.

16. See "How to Quench the Spirit without Really Trying: An Essay on Institutional Sexism" and "The Status of Women in the American Church," *Church and Society*, 63 (September–October 1972) 25–37.

17. I Cor. 11:3; Eph. 5:22–23.

18. Ignatius of Antioch, Epistles to the Magnesians and to the Trallians.

19. The by now famous phrase "spiritual lesbianism" seems to have come from Canon Joseph Wittkofski of the conservative Foundation for Christian Theology; See *Convention Daily*, Louisville, Ky., Oct. 6 (1973), p. 4.

20. Paul Van Buren, "Who's in Charge Here?" *The Witness*, August 1972, p. 12.

PART TWO
Strange Bedfellows: Women and Other Aliens

Witches and Jews:
The Demonic Alien
in Christian Culture

I HAVE ALREADY REFERRED IN TWO OF THE PRECEDING CHAP-
ters to the phenomenon of witchcraft. But because so little is known of the subject, and because of its historical
importance, I want to discuss it now in greater detail.

The witch hunts that broke out in the later Middle
Ages, increasing in fury until the end of the seventeenth
century, comprise indeed one of the most hidden chapters in Western history. The victims were overwhelmingly
female. Their numbers during the thirty decades of the
most intense persecution are estimated at about one million[1]—a holocaust, given the inefficient methods of execution relative to modern times. Modern scholars seldom
devote more than a few sentences to the fact that most
of the victims were women.[2] Yet the theoreticians of the
witch hunts make explicit connections between diabolism and what they regard as the moral, psychological,
and biological "nature" of women. In this chapter I will
summarize the phenomenon of witch belief, its transformation into a Satan cult, and will proffer some reasons as
to why women were its stereotypic villains.

THE OLD TESTAMENT AND EARLY CHRISTIAN
BACKGROUND OF WITCH BELIEF

The idea that witches are women is widespread and
older than Christianity. Witch hunters quoted with satisfaction the talmudic saying that "where there are many
women there are many witches" and elevated into law
the Old Testament text: "You shall not permit a sorcer-
ess to live" (Exod. 22:18).[3] In the Old Testament the ped-

dler of charms, potions, and occult knowledge is often female, e.g., the medium of Endor whom Saul consulted (I Sam. 28:7–25). There are various reasons why women appear in these roles. One is that the mysteries with which the witch deals—birth and death, the chthonic realm, medicine, midwifery—all flow out of women's roles as mother, cook, pharmacist, doctor, symbol of the maternal and earth powers. Second, the exclusion of women from the official priesthoods that sanction male hunting, scribal and kingly power pushes women's charisms into the unsanctioned realm, where they are seen as subversive and occult, yet to be resorted to when normal channels fail.

Judaism and other classical systems of religious law emphasized the demonic character of women by stigmatizing menstruation as "unclean." This concept is not to be explained by secular hygienic rationalizations. Originally the idea of uncleanness is highly magical. Mother's blood is a dangerous negative substance. The superstitions that milk sours, grass withers, and cows abort in the presence of a menstruating woman, that males dare not come near her without peril to their health and potency reveal the magical character of the concept of the "curse." In folklore menstrual blood is a central ingredient in magic potions. Christians believed that Jews used it in the poisons that caused the black death. Witch *maleficia* has deep roots in this demonization of female sexuality. But as I indicated earlier, originally these taboos had a positive sacral character.[4] However, when maternal power was repressed in patriarchy, mother's blood, the blood mystery of femaleness, was marginalized, its magic was regarded as polluting and evil. The suppression of female sacrality operated in antithesis to the sacralization of male power in the official scribal and priestly classes and the exclusion of women from their sacred precincts. Christianity inherited and enshrined this same antithesis between the purity of male sanctuaries and female uncleanness.

Beyond this heritage from Judaism, Christianity added developments of its own that heightened the association of women and the demonic. The New Testament is a world gripped by demons. Jesus himself operates as an exorcist healer. Like other apocalyptic sectarians, Christians divided the world, human and angelic, into two opposite camps, the Kingdom of Light and the Kingdom of Darkness. The New Testament locates traditional Jews in the devil's camp.[5] As the Gospel of John (8:44) says:

> You are of your father the devil, and your will is to do your father's desires. He was a murderer from the beginning, . . . a liar and the father of lies.

The book of Revelation calls the Jews "a synagogue of Satan (2:9), a term which the Church would also use for heretics and witches.

As the Church moved into the Greco-Roman world, pagan religion was also perceived as demonic. In much Christian theology pagan gods are demons. As Christianity moved north into Europe in its mission, it continued to view the religions of the peoples it sought to convert as diabolism. The conquest of the cults of paganism was the conquest of Satan worship. A split was created between the circle of light represented by the Church and the alien darkness not yet conquered by Christ. This antithesis was also identified with the ascetic dualism between flesh and spirit. The Children of Light mortify the flesh and aspire to the "angelic life." The Children of Darkness are typified as "carnal." All aliens tend to be seen as libidinous. The Church Fathers, especially John Chrysostom, established a view of the Jews as orgiastics.[6] This libel was also to be attached to heretics. But the witch was to be the ultimate fantasy of the demonic orgiastic.

Ascetic Christianity also identified the split between carnality and spirituality with femaleness and maleness. Females, too, were believed capable of spirituality. But, as I indicated in earlier chapters, the identification of the female with the fleshly side of the dualism created an asymmetrical evaluation of women in relation to men. Males were "naturally spiritual." Women, both in creation and through the fall, were representatives of "carnality." They must transcend, not only their bodily, but their "feminine" nature in order to be saved. Even so they could exercise their spiritual gifts only behind the veil of seclusion. Even the virgin must be subject to male "headship." Sexually they symbolized the enemy of the "angelic community." Medieval scholasticism deepened patristic misogynism. The Church also carried over the Jewish legendary tradition which ascribed the very existence of demons to the seduction of angels by women. The apocryphal expansion of the story of Genesis 6:1–4 also established the possibility of carnal intercourse between women and fallen angels.[7] Thus, in Christian theology, the female nature fell on the negative side of the dualisms between flesh and spirit, demons and angels.

EUROPEAN FOLK MAGIC AND THE CHURCH

Organized witch persecution, however, is not a phenomenon of the patristic period or early Middle Ages, but of the late medieval and Reformation eras. To explain this fact one must first clarify the relationship between the folk beliefs and magic practices which actually existed in village life and the theoretical superstructure created by the Church's inquest which interpreted and systematized these beliefs in the form of a "satanic cult." Scholars who have carefully studied the records of the witch trials find little evidence that covens existed or that witches actually functioned in organized groups.[8] The ideas that the witches were an organized devil religion, that they possessed leadership and organization (the coven), that they held nocturnal cultic gatherings (the Sabbat), that they possessed rituals (the *osculum profanum* of the devil, repudiation of the Christian for a demonic creed, profane meal and orgy)—such ideas were the manufacture of the inquisitors' imaginations.

It is difficult, however, to distinguish clearly between the original folk foundations and the superstructure created by the inquisitors because this theory was constantly fed back into the imaginations of the lay people, generating cultic groups that modeled themselves after the official theory. Much of this belongs to the seventeenth century and even later to the nineteenth-century revival. Rituals, such as the Black Mass, were not even a part of medieval witch theory, but were created in the late seventeenth century.[9] Twentieth-century witch fanciers, such as Margaret Murray, have interpreted witchcraft as a pre-Christian matriarchal religion.[10] Some feminists have adopted this view and have come to see witches as members of a dissident feminine religion against the Church. Any effort to achieve a just view of the phenomenon of witchcraft in these periods must clear away many layers of tendentious ideology.

It seems possible to distinguish at least three types of interrelated ideas and practices which were actually a part of the folk data upon which the clerical theorists built their concept of witchcraft as a satanic religion. First, there were strata of survivals of European paganisms. These were no single religion, and no official priesthood remained for it. When the Church conquered the various European peoples over the course of a thousand years, it was most concerned to destroy the official cult and priesthood that sanctified political power and to transfer the fidelity of the leadership class to the Christian Church. What survived, then, was not this official cult, but that stratum of religion that belongs to village daily life, the rituals of the home and farming life, which the people carry on for themselves. Group observances, especially those tied with hunting and farming—village dances, festivals, harvest homes, often with much drinking and sexual excitement—gave village life a way of celebrating the victories of survival and relaxing from the tensions of labor and adversity. For official Christianity there was no doubt that the gods of these earlier religions were "demons." Yet, in practice, the Church was content to erect a superstructure of Christianity and bring village life superficially under the aegis of the Church. Even when churchmen refer to these village practices, they seldom know the popular terminology. As men of Latin education, they typically refer to it through names and myths drawn from classical literature.[11]

A second type of phenomenon we might call "folk magic." The idea that the earth, air, and underworld were populated by a host of spirits was taken for granted by all. These spirits might be malevolent or benevolent. They might be tricksters but amenable to bribery. Such ideas survive in European tales of fairies, sprites, leprechauns, ogres, giants, and dwarfs. The "little people" could take animal form. This was probably the source of the Church's idea of the witch's familiar. For the villagers, life was a series of points of inexplicable tension, where malevolent forces might hold sway and where it was necessary to arm oneself with various potions, charms, and amulets to fend off their influence or direct favorable influences upon one's own projects. Birth, sickness, death, weather changes, planting and reaping, accidents, mysterious changes of all kinds—these were the occasion for various magical practices. Many of these practices were not without real potency, sometimes because there was genuine medical or scientific basis for them, garnered over millennia of experience,[12] sometimes simply because one believed in it. Curses were believed to be genuinely effective. A person who believed herself or himself cursed might go home and die.

Women had a primordial role in such magical lore. Particularly the old woman living alone seems to have cultivated such knowledge, partly because it provided her with a "profession" through which she could offset her economic insecurity. In older urbanized settings the urban witch survived from classical times. This type of witch might be an old harlot who acted as go-between for lovers, purveyor of love charms, beauty aids, poisons, and contraceptives.[13] In the rural setting the magic of the witch operated in the spheres of natural crises. She was the midwife and folk doctor, herbal pharmacist and purveyor of charms to protect one from malevolence, either natural or directed from other persons, or to direct retribution back at others. Such a person would be resented only when one perceived her to be responsible for misfortunes. But one also relied on her to provide the lore of healing and protection.[14] Such a woman must have been in a vulnerable position, since her "trade" occupied the connecting point between all the uncertainties and hostilities that afflicted village life. The villagers did not condemn her for being a witch, since all practiced and believed in magic as a basic form of manipulating the problems of daily life. They would condemn her only when they saw her as a "bad witch." The inquisitioners' violation of this distinction overthrew the basic economy of village hex-practice.

A third related type of data also came to be interpreted by the inquisitors as "Satanism." This is what one might call folk superstition. Two kinds of ideas are worth mentioning because of the interpretation given them in the clerical theory. One is the idea that people can ride out at night on magical conveyances. Nocturnal agricultural celebrations may have contributed to the concept of the Sabbat to which the witch rides. But the idea of night-riding itself may originate simply from a literal interpretation of dreams. In American Indian religion, dream adventures are taken very seriously and much valued. Drugs and special rigors are used to induce them. European villagers may have had similar ways of seeking dream adventures.[15]

A second important folk belief is the interpretation of

nocturnal sexual fantasies as intercourse with demons. Medieval Jews, as well as Christians, shared the interpretation of sexual fantasies as intercourse with *incubi* and *succubi*. Male wetdreams were regarded as intercourse with a female demon called "Lilith." Such experiences were regarded as dangerous. The person sleeping alone should take special precautions against such nocturnal visitations.[16] This was the idea which the inquisitors would magnify into the dogma of the satanic pact between the witch and the devil. Folk belief did not regard these demons as *the* devil, but simply as everyday, somewhat dangerous spirits. But the inquisitors had a grip, here, upon a basic root in everyday experience which could be enormously magnified through guilt. Since everyone might experience such night eroticism, once this experience was interpreted as intercourse with the devil, people's imaginations could be invaded by heightened fear. They would come to interpret their guilty night fantasies in this way, under duress of torture and determined questioning, or even experience their dreams this way in advance.

Such interiorizing of the inquisitors' doctrines into people's actual experience should not surprise us. Today, the psychoanalyst has in some ways, replaced the inquisitors as the official bully who forces women to interpret their dreams in terms of a priori male doctrines. The high point of witch hunting took place after the invention of printing. This meant that ideas such as the Sabbat, demonic intercourse, the *osculum profanum*, originally embedded in clerical manuals written in Latin, could be popularly disseminated through woodcuts.[17] Everyone could now see what such things looked like and begin to experience their fantasies or imagine those of their neighbors accordingly. So, in understanding the ability of inquisitors to wring from their victims convincing confessions that conformed to the official theories, one must not just suppose that these were imposed by

torture. One must also reckon with the earlier folk beliefs, plus the ability of the official theory to shape those
folk beliefs into the new interpretation through cultural
suggestion.

The concept of carnal intercourse with the devil was
central to the inquisitors' view of the witch as a "satan-
ist" who had entered into a formal pact with the devil,
sealed by intercourse. It was by wringing a confession of
demonic intercourse from the witch that the witch could
be condemned as an apostate who had renounced God
and his Church and given herself to the devil.[18] Although
folk belief gave equal place to the male experience with
succubi, this idea faded beside the basic concept of the
witch as a female who has intercourse with a male devil.
This seems to have been so because the devil was seen,
by the Church, as male, so his paramours must be female (the devil is a strict heterosexual!) and also because women were regarded by the celibate clergymen
as the exemplars of insatiable carnal lust. In the *Malleus
Maleficarum* (pt. I, sec. 6) which sums up three centuries
of official theory, the entire heritage of both high and low
misogynism is evoked to show why it is that witches appear primarily in the female sex.

> When a woman thinks alone, she thinks evil. . . . I have
> found a woman more bitter than death, and a good woman
> subject to carnal lust. They are more impressionable than
> men and more ready to receive the influence of the disem-
> bodied spirit. . . . They have slippery tongues. . . . Since
> they are weak, they find an easy and secret manner of vindi-
> cating themselves in witchcraft. They are feebler both in
> mind and body. It is not surprising that they should come
> more under the spell of witchcraft. As regards intellect or un-
> derstanding of spiritual things, they seem to be of a different
> nature than men. . . . Women are intellectually like children.
> . . . And it should be noted that there was a defect in the for-
> mation of the first woman, since she was formed from the
> bent rib, the rib of the breast which is bent in the contrary di-
> rection to a man. . . . And since through the first defect in
> their intelligence, they are always more prone to abjure the

faith, so through their second defect of inordinate passions, they search for, brood over and inflict various vengeances, either by witchcraft or some other means. Wherefore it is no wonder that so great a number of witches exist in this sex. . . . Women have weaker memories, and it is a natural vice in them not to be disciplined, but to follow their own impulses without any sense of what is due. . . . She is a liar by nature. . . . Let us consider her gait, posture and habit, in which she is vanity of vanities. . . . Woman is a wheedling and secret enemy. For the sake of fulfilling their lusts they consort even with devils.

The Dominican inquisitors take for granted the Thomistic definition of woman as a "misbegotten male," defective intellectually, morally, and biologically in the order of nature, and the subject of inordinate lust in the disorder of the fall. Various biblical stories are adduced to prove these misogynist statements, climaxed—as noted above—by the etymology of the word *femina* as meaning lacking in faith. Apostasy is shown to be inherent in the very nature of that being which is feminine. Woman as sexual threat dominates the treatise. The writers conclude the section on why witches are female by declaring that "nothing is so insatiable as the mouth of the womb" and offering up thanksgiving to God because, through the incarnation of his Son in the male sex, males have been preserved from so great an evil as witchcraft. This statement is particularly startling, since it comes close to using the maleness of Jesus to justify the exclusion of women from the fruits of redemption, i.e., the possibility of being Christians. The very word for witch in the *Malleus* is feminine, and the witch is referred to throughout as a female. This misogynist pattern was not peculiar to the Dominicans' work. It was standard to refer to witches as women in the witch hunter's treatises and to include a section showing, from the "nature" of women, why witches are female. This pattern is found equally in sixteenth- and seventeenth-century treatises written by Protestants.[19]

The witch craze must then be seen as a harvest of the Christian traditions of misogynism and sexual repression. Women, moreover, were more vulnerable to the invasion of their imaginations by these theories about them than were other persecuted groups, such as Jews. Jews were an organized religious people who had their own alternative self-understanding. However much they might shrink behind the ghetto walls raised around them by Christendom, they had an internal cohesion and identity to protect their minds from the fantasies projected upon them by Christians, such as well-poisoning, drinking the blood of murdered Christian boys on Passover, or stabbing Hosts to perform evil magic. The witches had no alternative community to protect their self-understanding. Only a strong individual could resist the pressure to conform her self-image to the prescribed interpretation. Such self-determination would be regarded as itself evidence of witchcraft. Only a woman aided by the devil would be able to refuse assent to the demanded answers, especially under torture. A woman brought for questioning was condemned in advance willy-nilly. She would be condemned either by her confession or by her refusal to confess. The very nature of confessions under torture created a double bind. This is blatantly so in tortures such as "swimming" a witch, in which the woman was thrown, manacled, into a pond. If she floated she was a witch; if she sank she was innocent.

THE DEVELOPMENT OF WITCH PERSECUTION

The village customs later to be interpreted as "satanism" were mostly ignored by churchmen in the earlier Middle Ages (sixth to eleventh centuries). In the ninth century Charlemagne made it a crime to kill a witch.[20] Canon law endorsed a skeptical view of the literal reality of such ideas as night flying.[21] The Church in this era seemed confident of its civilizing mission. But in the twelfth century, with the development of more complex settled cultures, heretical movements arose, challenging the leadership of the Church. The Waldensians and Franciscans attacked the luxury of the hierarchy. The Albigensians proclaimed an extreme dualism between the God of Light and the God of Darkness, between spiritual and carnal being. They practiced a violent asceticism and regarded themselves as the Children of Light, the Catholic Church as the Kingdom of Satan.

The Church responded to these challenges with an internal crusade, massacring large numbers of the Albigensian population. The crusaders began their marches to the East at this same period. In connection with both types of crusades successive pogroms broke out against the Jews. Many of the ideas later projected upon witches, such as nocturnal orgies and child sacrifice, were directed by the Inquisition first against heretics. The belief that witches belonged to organized sects seems particularly to have derived from the earlier experience with heretics. Witches were even called by such names as Waudenses and Gazari, which identify them with Waldensians and Cathari.[22]

By the end of the thirteenth century the Inquisition had broken the back of these earlier heresies. But it began to perceive yet another more insidious heresy concealed beneath them. This was identified as witchcraft. By defining witchcraft as an apostate satanic cult, the inquisitors were able to include it within their authority, contrary to the earlier canonical rules. A new, more intensive, crusade was launched in many of the areas already scoured for heretics. It seems that many of the folk customs which had previously been ignored by the high culture of the church leaders had now come to their attention because of this intense activity of local investigation. The first stage of witchcraft persecution functioned as a purge by the orthodox Catholic culture of the ethnically distinct folkways of villagers and highlanders.

During the first hundred years of witch trials, males number about equally with women. Indeed the first major witch trial (1306–1314), was a political tool for expropriating the banking business of the Knights Templar[23] (the French king having previously expropriated that of the Jews and the Lombards). However, the official theory defined the witch as generically female. The accused came to be predominantly female in the major witch hunts from the late fifteenth through the seventeenth centuries.[24] The rise of witch hunts from 1380–1480 coincides with a spreading paranoia in European society. New pogroms and outbreaks of mass hysteria greeted crises such as the black death. The late Middle Ages is a world gripped by the image of the devil. The Jew comes to be depicted as a kind of devil incarnate, while the witch is the free-floating anxiety symbol of diabolic femaleness.

The *Malleus Maleficarum*, published in 1486, summed up a century of official theory by inquisitors and theologians. The papal bull *Summis desiderantes*, issued in 1484, empowered the two Dominicans, Heinrich Krämer and Jacob Sprenger, to carry the witch hunts into North Germany. The papal bull itself locates the *maleficia* of witches primarily in the sexual realm, such as causing abortions, sterility, contraception, castration, impotency, as well as the infecundity of flocks and fields.[25] The *Malleus* became the definitive document of witch persecution. Its view of the evil deeds of witches is dominated by sexual fantasy. No less than six of the seven chapters on the nature, discovery, and processing of witches are heavily sexual. The inquisitors unburden themselves with various tales about the deeds done by witches. Witches are in the habit of stealing the male member. One young man, suspecting that this had been the result of the activity of a certain witch, went to her and insisted that she return it. She confessed her deed and led him to a tree where he found a nest filled with penises moving about like birds. She told him he might take whichever he chose, but not to choose the "big one," which belonged to the village priest.[26]

The methods of torture also reflect this preoccupation with sexual prurience in witch persecution. In diabolic intercourse the devil was believed to place a mark on the witch as the sign that he or she was his property. In women this was normally on the breast or genitals. Small protrusions on the body were also believed to be teats by which the witch nursed her familiar. Witches were stripped and shaved. Their bodies were searched and the sensitive parts pricked in search of these supposed bodily proofs of demonic relations.

Witch hunters, both Catholic and Protestant, insisted that no distinction can be made between a white and a black witch, between the witch who does good and the one who causes harm. All are to be killed, because the sin of witchcraft does not consist in evil deeds, but in the act of apostasy to the devil, which makes magic acts possible. In this decree the witch hunters differed from the folk practice that may have generated particular accusations, and they turned existing folk belief into a general assault upon everyone connected with such practices that was potentially endless. The revival of torture, with the re-establishment of Roman law in late medieval jurisprudence, also contributed greatly to the escalation of the trials. Torture allowed accusations to proliferate to epidemic proportions, because once a witch confessed under torture, she would be tortured again to divulge the names of neighbors seen at the Sabbat. When various names were blurted out by the unfortunates, these would be summoned and the process would begin again. By this process the Bishop-Prince of Trier almost decimated the population of many villages between 1587 and 1593, following his expulsion of Protestants and Jews. He had some 368 witches from twenty-two villages burned, leaving several villages with only one female member. In the

early seventeenth century the Lutheran witch hunter
Benedict Carpzov boasted of having burned no less
than twenty thousand persons himself, while Nicolas
Rémy declared that he had burned several thousand in
Lorraine between 1581 and 1591.[27]

In England, where torture was disallowed for most of
this period, the numbers of witches executed remained
small, perhaps less than one thousand in the three centuries of the craze. The accusations remained close to
actual village tensions and hostilities and did not proliferate into general purges of large populations. The general picture of the accusations goes something like this.
An old woman, in straitened circumstances, was impor-
tuning her neighbors for help. Her hostility to her neighbors mounted when they refused her some request.
Later mysterious misfortunes afflicted the neighbors, and
the old woman was perceived as taking vengeance
through witchcraft. The English trials allow us to catch a
faithful picture of the actual folk beliefs and the economic tensions that so often made the impoverished old
woman its victim. The theoretical superstructure created
by the inquisitors, such as night flights, Sabbats, intercourse with the devil, and the *osculum profanum* are
generally absent from these trials.[28]

At the beginning of the sixteenth century the new hu-
manism seemed to be dispelling witch hunting. But, then,
in the era of the religious wars that followed Luther's
break with the medieval Church, the hunts were revived,
becoming steadily worse until the middle of the seventeenth century, when they again began to decline, all but
dying out by the end of the century—although an occasional witch was burned in Scotland, the Basque highlands, and other areas of entrenched belief into the
eighteenth century. The famous trials in Salem, Massachusetts, took place in the 1690s. In this entire period,
not only Dominican inquisitors, but rival courts of bishops, Protestant and Catholic princes, and local magis-

trates tried and executed witches. No critic of witchcraft was tolerated until the last decade of the seventeenth century. It became a dogma that those who cast doubt on the reality of witches were themselves agents of the devil.[29]

This revival of witch persecution coincides closely with aggressive sectarian conflict between Protestants and Catholics. As Protestant militancy spread in some areas and then retreated in others, before the counteroffensive of the Jesuits, witch hunts followed the expulsion of the leaders of the rival faith. Calvinists and Lutherans enthusiastically endorsed the medieval view of the devil and his human cohorts, and regarded witches as papists, while Catholics included Protestantism in the traditional identification of witches and heretics.[30] Witch hunts spread in an atmosphere of renewed religious ideological warfare, each side seeking to terrorize the local population into submission to its orthodoxies. The fear created by an unfamiliar world of economic and political upheavals and the breakdown of a unified ecclesiastical authority suggested that demonic forces had gripped the whole world. The witch was the scapegoat of this inchoate social fear.

The fading of witch beliefs and trials as the seventeenth century came to an end is usually explained by the penetration of a more rational scientific world-view into the general culture. But there seems to be another element at work that caused witch trials to proliferate and then break down and fade away in one area or another. From such studies we can guess something of the social psychology of the selection of victims. Particular misfortunes and hostilities might be the occasion for the beginning of accusations. The use of torture turned the sequence of accusations into an epidemic. The economic motivation entered in, and a greedy judge was tempted to extend the accusations to wealthy members of the community, since the property of the condemned was confiscated. A magistrate or prominent person began to object to the trials, and he himself became included in the accused. When such prominent persons were accused, the credibility of the confessions extracted under torture broke down and influential public opinion began to suspect that the previous confessions did not represent real experiences. In other words, the credibility of the witch as scapegoat for social anxieties depended on maintaining the stereotype of the witch as an old woman, i.e., a vulnerable and unprotected person. When this social category was too greatly violated and persons of greater social credibility were drawn into the net, then the reliability of the witch hunter's processes was thrown into question and the hunt subsided.[31]

WITCHES AND JEWS: THE PARANOID PATTERN IN CHRISTIAN CULTURE

There is a peculiar parallelism between the figure of the witch and that of the Jew in late medieval imagination. Both the witch and the Jew came to be seen as agents of the devil, representing a demonic plot to subvert the power of God and his Church in the world. Full-fledged persecutions of witches and pogroms against Jews seldom took place simultaneously. The Jew had been expelled from France and England by the fourteenth century, but communities remained in Germany. Spain, which had burned witches earlier, was preoccupied with the persecution of Jews and Marranos in the later Middle Ages. The two figures seemed to operate as alternative symbols of a demonic subversion of Christendom.[32]

The image of the Jew as a demonic alien was similar in many ways to that of the witch. The Jew also came to be seen as a sorcerer who defies and blasphemes the faith of the Church. The Jew was seen as a devil worshiper, equipped with horns, claws, and tail, riding on the satanic goat. Like the witch, the Jew was believed to steal

the Eucharist and to perform other blasphemous carica-
tures of Catholic rituals.[33] Here we see that the black
magic of witches and Jews was defined in antithetical
relation to the legitimate magic of the Church. The magic
view of Catholic sacramental acts was the nexus within
which the ideas of diabolic magic were defined.

There is a certain interchange of images between
Jews and witches whereby each is defined by being associated with the proven demonic character of the other.
Witches are mocked on the way to execution by being
exposed in the pointed hat that the Church made Jews
wear. Terms, such as the *Sabbat* and *synagogue* for
witches' gatherings, are drawn from the Church's demonization of Jewish worship. Even more peculiar is the
way Jews become defamed by being associated with the
demonic properties of the female. In the anti-Semitic lore
developed in Spain during the mass persecution of Jews
and Marranos in the fifteenth century, it is said that the
Jewish male has been cursed for his refusal to accept
Christ by being afflicted with menstruation.[34] Menstrual
blood, as we have noted, was a typical ingredient of demonic brews, along with boiled children, hideous sub-
stances like reptiles and offal, and sacramental sub-
stances. Jews, like witches and heretics, were seen as
practitioners of child immolation and drinking the blood
of a Christian boy on Passover. Plagues and mysterious
deaths were attributed to their poisonings. Jews, like
women, were seen as impious, faithless, contumacious,
and lusty.

The image of the witch was that of an old woman,
while that of the Jew was that of an old man, usually rabbis and elders. How could two groups so obviously disparate in their actual sociology come to be the recipients
of such similar stereotypes in medieval thought? This
cannot be explained by any similarities between them.
Although both were oppressed groups in Christian society, the self-consciousness of the male leadership of the

Jewish community bore little similarity to that of elderly women from the bottom of Christian society. The similar stereotypes must be explained, rather, by the fact that both were projections from the consciousness of the Christian male leadership groups. The clergy saw themselves as the masters of the redemption won by Christ, and regarded Jews, witches, and heretics as agents of the devil's plot to subvert their rule. All these groups acquired similar characteristics as devil worshipers, orgiastics, and magicians.

Although our account of the witch has to do with Christian culture, the myth of Satan and his human agents did not end with secularism. The myth of a demonic plot against the Christian West continued into the modern era, particularly in the myth of the international Jewish conspiracy. The anti-Semitic hatred that revived in the late nineteenth century, culminating in Nazism, translated medieval Jew-baiting into secular, racial form. Its key document, the *Protocols of the Elders of Zion*, still preserved the demonological fantasy of apocalypticism. According to the *Protocols* Jewish leadership formed a secret worldwide cabal, in existence since the death of Christ, pledged to its leader, the devil, to overthrow Christendom and establish the reign of the Antichrist.[35] This fantasy was, in turn, the foundation of the derivative myth of the Jewish-Communist conspiracy which used the *Protocols* to blame the so-called Jewish conspiracy for the Russian Revolution in 1917.

Although the power of various communist states is real, but hardly unified, while that of the *Protocols of Zion* was a fabrication, the psychology of anticommunism, especially among right-wing Christians, exhibits the paranoid character which caused observers to compare the McCarthy era with "witch hunts." The archetypal "communist" of the Right and the FBI (often seen as a Jew) is an invisible, yet almost omnipotent demonic figure who plots against the Christian West on behalf of the Kingdom of Darkness. His tools are not only political subversion and "selling secrets to the enemy," but also undermining the moral fiber of Christendom. This paranoid myth is by no means dead today. In 1973 Bethany Press in Minneapolis published *The Bible, the Supernatural and the Jews* by McCandish Philips, which featured on its cover the flames of hell arising from the infernal regions, encompassing a broken tablet inscribed with the Hebrew ‫ש‬. The author argues that Jews, being God's chosen people, become far more powerfully evil than gentiles when they fall away from God. With this theological assumption, the author goes on to blame satanism, drugs, rock music, dissent, and the breakdown of traditional morality in the youth counterculture upon the superior capacity of the Jew for evil.[36]

We can recognize a somewhat similar concatenation of social and sexual elements in the medieval and the modern forms of paranoia. The persecuted group is seen as breaking down the established authority of the social consensus and also as flouting its sexual morality. It matters very little that the Jew was hardly orgiastic in the Middle Ages, that the heretics persecuted by the Church were themselves practitioners of rigid asceticism, or that official communism is highly puritanical. Invariably these agents of the powers of evil are seen by the dominant society both as blasphemers of the received faith and order of society, and also as people who indulge in lascivious sexual practices and infect the rest of society with spreading debauchery. What we seem to find here is a link between the social and the psychological sides of oppression, a link between social domination and sexual repression. Both kinds of oppression are extrojected upon a scapegoat figure who is seen as the agent of social subversion and sexual rebellion. Sexual repression fantasizes the "alien" as one who practices unbridled debauchery of every kind. Women were the direct victim of this paranoia in the late Middle Ages, as women are the prime object both of social domination and of sexual repression. But in the modern ideologies of anti-Semitism and anticommunism one finds also an antiliberalism which seeks to counteract, among other things, ideas of female liberation and restore the traditional subjugation of women.[37]

However widely different the phenomena of these movements, a similar psychology is found in them that has peculiar roots in the Christian self-image. The Christian traditionally believes that the messianic event of final salvation has already taken place. The devil has been defeated and a privileged circle of salvation set up in the Church and Christendom. But since this doctrine of achieved salvation could not reckon with the actuality of social justice, it was turned inward and located as an invisible grace whose primary expression was bodily negation. Christian realized eschatology was reified in a culture of sexual repression. The traditional social subjugation of women, lower classes, and servants could then be justified anew. Eschatology separated from history becomes a socially conservative, rather than a liberating, force.

The perfectionism inculcated by the doctrine of fulfilled messianism means also that the Christian Church loses a certain capacity for self-criticism which was part of the prophetic tradition which looked for a fulfillment that was still to come. When social and natural catastrophes threatened the Christian confidence in its historic victory over evil, this could not be internalized in the form of soul-searching for the causes of infidelity within the Church itself, as has been the case with Judaism. Since the Church, at least objectively and institutionally, represented the completion of Christ's salvation, blame for collective evil tended to be externalized. The Christians tended to project the causes of evil outward, locating it in a demonic "conspiracy" surrounding the people of God, which was personified in religious or social aliens, in heretics, or in the revolt of the "flesh," i.e., serfs, women, beneath its "head." Women and Jews for centuries were two scapegoats of this paranoid tendency of Christian culture.[38] Later, with the advent of colonialism, the Blacks became a new model of both the "pagan" and the bestial. In the next chapter I will explore the special relationship of sexism and racism that developed in the United States.

Notes

1. It is difficult to estimate the numbers killed during the four centuries of major witchcraft persecutions. Some scholars use the figure "between 100,000 and one million." But the first figure is far too low when one begins to count up the numbers cited from the different regions. Leo Bonfanti has added to these figures an estimation of the large numbers that died in prison without execution, and has come up with the figure of "between 1 and 9 million" (*The Witch-craft Hysteria of 1692*, New England Historical Series, p. 9). This latter figure was used by A. Dworkin in "What Were Those Witches Really Brewing," *Ms.*, April 1974, pp. 52ff. But to speak of "nine million females," as she and feminists who have followed her figure have done, is inflated and ignores the percentage of males that must be included in this figure. The figure of "about one million," cited by various scholars of witch persecution, therefore, is no more than a fairly safe guess.

2. For example Alan McFarlane offers much evidence for the relation of the stereotype of woman as witch and the socio-economic condition of witches, but he discusses only the factors of age and poverty and ignores its relation to sex (*Witchcraft in Tudor and Stuart England* [London: Routledge and Kegan Paul, 1970], pp. 161, 148–56, 205).

3. Alexander Roberts, *A Treatise on Witchcraft* (1616) in *Witches and Witch-hunters* (Wakefield, Yorks: S. R. Publishers, 1971). 7th proposition.

4. See Ruth Underhill, "Woman's Power," in *Red Man's Religion* (Chicago: University of Chicago Press, 1965).

5. See Edward Langton, *Essentials of Demonology: A Study of Jewish-Christian Doctrine* (London: Epworth, 1942), and Samson Eitrem, *Some Notes on the Demonology of the New Testament* (Oslo: Symbolae Osloenses 12, 1950).

6. John Chrysostom, *Eight Sermons against the Jews*, Migne, *P.G.* 48; cols. 843–942; see R. Ruether, *Faith and Fratricide* (New York: Seabury, 1974), chap. 3.

7. Bernard Prusak, "Woman: Seductive Siren and Source of

Sin?" in *Religion and Sexism*, ed. R. Ruether (New York: Simon and Schuster, 1974), pp. 89–116.

8. McFarlane, *op. cit.,* p. 10, and H. C. E. Midelfort, *Witch Hunting in South West Germany, 1563–84* (Stanford: Stanford University Press, 1972), p. 1.

9. J. B. Russell, *Witchcraft in the Middle Ages* (Ithaca: Cornell University Press, 1972), pp. 24, 296, n. 12.

10. Margaret Murray, *God of the Witches* (2nd ed.; London: Oxford University Press, 1952); *The Witch Cult in Western Europe* (London: Oxford University Press, 1921). The use of the Murray thesis by feminist theology can be seen in Mary Daly, *Beyond God the Father* (Boston: Beacon Press, 1973), pp. 63, 66, 147, 148, 150.

11. Russell, *op. cit.,* pp. 45–62.

12. John Middleton, ed., *Magic, Witchcraft and Curing* (Garden City, N.Y.: Doubleday, 1967). Also, Barbara Ehrenreich and Deirdre English, *Witches, Midwives and Nurses* (New York: Feminist Press, 1973).

13. J. Caro Baroja, *The World of Witches* (Chicago: University of Chicago Press, 1964), pp. 101–2.

14. Thomas Forbes, *The Midwife and the Witch* (New Haven: Yale University Press, 1966).

15. Russell, *op. cit.,* p. 38.

16. Raphael Patai, "Lilith," in *The Hebrew Goddess* (Ktav, 1967), pp. 207–45.

17. Alan Kors and Edward Peter, *Witchcraft in Europe, 1100–1700* (Philadelphia: University of Pennsylvania Press, 1972), p. 18.

18. R. Masters, *Eros and Evil: The Sexual Pathology of Witchcraft* (New York: Julian Press, 1962).

19. E.g., Alexander Roberts, *A Treatise on Witchcraft* (1616), 7th proposition and James I, *Daemonologie* (Edinburgh, 1597), Bk. II, chap. V.

20. *Capitulatio de Partibus Saxoniae,* chap. 6.

21. Canon Episcopi, in H. C. Lea, *Materials Toward a History of Witchcraft* (Philadelphia: University of Pennsylvania Press, 1939), I: 178–82.

22. Russell, *op. cit.,* pp. 101–32.

23. *Ibid.,* pp. 194–98.

24. Midelfort, *op. cit.,* pp. 178–90.

25. Kors and Peter, *op. cit.*, pp. 107–12; extracted from G. L. Burr, *The Witch Persecutions: Translations and Reprints from Original Sources of European History* (Philadelphia: University of Pennsylvania Press, 1902), pp. 7–10.

26. *Malleus Maleficarum*, trans. Montague Summers (London: J. Rodker, 1928), sec. 7; see also H. R. Hays, *The Dangerous Sex: The Myth of Feminine Evil* (New York: Pocket Books, 1972), pp. 141–45.

27. H. R. Trevor-Roper, "The European Witchcraze in the 16th and 17th Centuries," in *The Crisis of the 17th Century* (New York: Harper & Row, 1968), pp. 117–23, 149, 152, 159.

28. McFarlane, *op. cit.*, pp. 147–77.

29. *Malleus Maleficarum*, pt. I, sec. 1, and pt. III, sec. 25; see Trevor-Roper, *op. cit.*, pp. 137–49. Selections from witchcraft critics Reginald Scot (1584), Michel de Montaigne, Spinoza, Alonso Salazar de Frias (1610), Thomas Hobbes (1651), Frederich Spee (1631), Pierre Bayle (1703), Balthasar Bekker (1691), and the recantation of the Salem jurors (1693) are found in Kors and Peter, *op. cit.*, pp. 311–78.

30. Trevor-Roper, *op. cit.*, pp. 137–46, 186–89.

31. This thesis is developed especially in Midelfort, *op. cit.*, chaps. 6 and 7.

32. Trevor-Roper, *op. cit.*, pp. 108–15.

33. Joshua Trachtenberg, *The Devil and the Jews* (New Haven: Yale University Press, 1943), pp. 196–216; see also "Demonic Alien" in Salo Baron, *Social and Religious History of the Jews* (New York: Columbia University Press, 1967), XI: 122ff.

34. Harriet Goldberg, "Two Medieval Commonplaces: Anti-Feminism and Anti-Semitism in Medieval Spanish Tradition"; paper presented at the 8th Annual Conference of the Center for Medieval and Early Renaissance Studies, May 4, 1974, Binghamton, N.Y.: to be published in *Jewish Culture in the Middle Ages* by the Center.

35. Norman Cohn, *Warrant for Genocide: The Myth of the Jewish World Conspiracy and the Protocols of the Elders of Zion* (New York: Harper & Row, 1966), pp. 21–59.

36. McCandish Philips, *The Bible, the Supernatural and the Jews* (Minneapolis, Minn.: Bethany Press, 1970; revised 1973), pp. 297–302 and *passim*.

37. On the misogynist aspect of the Nazi antithesis between

German and Jew, see G. Mosse, *The Crisis of German Ideology* (New York: Grosset and Dunlap, 1964), pp. 215–16. The thesis was developed earlier in Otto Weininger, *Sex and Character* (New York: Putnam, 1906), esp. pp. 301–30.

38. The relationship between realized eschatology and anti-Semitism is developed in R. Ruether, *Faith and Fratricide* (New York: Seabury, 1974), chap. 5 and *passim*.

Between the Sons of White and the Sons of Blackness: Racism and Sexism in America

ALTHOUGH THE TWO MOST IMPORTANT EXPRESSIONS OF LIBERA-tion theology to emerge in America in the late sixties have been black theology and feminist theology, an undeclared war is brewing between them. The white male-dominated seminaries first adjusted their self-absolutizing perspective slightly to find some crumbs for black studies. Later some began to divide these crumbs further to create an opposite corner for women's studies. Thereby these two expressions of criticism of the dominant social context of theological reflection and education were set up to compete with each other.

A ruling class typically tries to set suppressed groups at each other's throats. This could well be another instance unless blacks and women themselves begin to figure out how better to avoid the trap. Black caucuses, appearing a year or two earlier than the women's caucuses, have generally denied reciprocal solidarity with the women's movement. Women, both in the first women's movement that began before the Civil War, and in the civil rights movement in the 1960s, have begun their own analysis by perceiving an analogy between the situation of women and the situation of blacks. When they have seen their own concerns pushed aside in the movement for black (male) rights, they have tended to withdraw in hurt alienation. In the nineteenth century women's rights were discarded by white male legislators, who were (temporarily) forced by their constitutional traditions to enfranchise freed black males, but who had no intention of extending this to women, white or black. In the black power and black nationalist movements that

115

arose in the latter half of the 1960s, the negative reactions toward women's liberation have come from many black males themselves. Far from being open to the question of female oppression, the model of black liberation has appeared to be modeled after the super-male-chauvinist traditions.

Why this tension? Are these two causes actually quite unrelated or even contradictory? Are blacks correct in denying solidarity with the women's movement? Are feminists specious in comparing racism with sexism? In fact, racism and sexism have been closely interrelated historically, especially in the American South, but they have not been exactly parallel. Rather, we should recognize them as interstructural elements of oppression within the overarching system of white male domination. But this interstructuring of oppression by sex, race, and also class, creates intermediate tensions and alienations—between white women and black women, between black men and white women, and even between black men and black women. Each group tends to suppress the experience of its racial and sexual counterparts. The black movement talks as though ''blacks'' means black males. In so doing it conceals the tensions between black males and black females. The women's movement fails to integrate the experience of black and poor women, and so fails to see that much of what it means by female experience is confined to those women within the dominant class and race. Protests which arise from the oppression of poor blacks are harvested by middle-class blacks without noticing the discrepancy. Implicit and overt exploitation of these interstructural tensions becomes the way in which the white upper-class male elite retains its control, even while conceding tidbits to token members of these suppressed groups. Liberation movements need to understand the tensions that arise because of this interstructuring of different modes of oppression within the overarching system of racist elite patriarchalism.

To understand the roots of this clash we must review the results of plantation slavery in the American South, for it was out of this heritage that the black community emerged in America. American slavery depended not only on a rigidly racist anthropology that denied the humanity of black people, but also on a destruction of the black family and the structuring of black women into a system of white male sexual dominance, with all its pathological results for black-white sexual-racial relations.

The elite white patriarch ruled supreme, dominating a society divided by sex, race, and class. Within the interface of sex and race, white females and black females were made the opposite sides of each other. The white woman was the delicate ornament of the parlor, while the black woman was exploited for sex and labor in the kitchen. This required the suppression of the rights of the black male as husband, father, and householder. Some recent historical revisionists, using official slave records rather than the diaries and personal letters on which much slave history has been based, have challenged the view that slavery totally denied any marriage structure to blacks. But their conclusion from this that blacks under slavery lived in stable, patriarchal family units is a naïve rejection of the overwhelming record of personal experience.[1] Rather, what we must see in slavery as well as in the succeeding system of caste racism is a hypocrisy that was in some ways more destructive than a systemic structuring of blacks into some alternative form of family relations. Token gestures of marriage were often allowed, and the rhetoric of patriarchal marriage ethics held up to blacks as their model. But the slave family was unable to emulate this model in reality, since the black male could not earn respect as a father or householder, his sexual rights to his wife could be violated at any time, and the whole family disrupted at will by the slaveowner.

The dual identities imposed on white and black women

reflect what we have defined above as the classical Christian schizophrenia toward the female. The white woman represented the asexual ideal of virginal feminity. She was a secular version of the virgin mother, chaste and innocent of sexual feeling; the shining image of pure womanhood before whom southern chivalric society knelt and offered up its Holy Grail. A cloying repressiveness on the level of mind and feelings surrounded her. The black woman paid the price of the white double standard. Black women were expected to be available to white males of the master class and could be punished severely if they refused the white male's advances. Worse punishment awaited the black male who intervened to protect his wife or sister.

The mulatto children of black women continued to be slaves. How widespread it was to select a few strapping black males to act as studs is unclear, but the black group was seen as the reproductive source of more slave property for the master. The black male may have been the greater psychological casualty of this system. The black woman ruled the cabin and provided the continuity for the black family. Without clear paternity the black child often could only look to its mother as source of identity. The black male was humiliated as male, husband, father, and householder, since the sole patriarch of the plantation was the white master. In the perfunctory marriage ceremonies that were allowed, it was customary to refer to the black female as a "woman" and the black man as a "boy." [2]

White ideology alternated between seeing blacks as subhuman beasts and seeing them as permanent children. Its rhetoric typically denied adult status to the black male. It is a mistake to speak of this system as matriarchal. The black family was female centered only in the sense that, in a society in which the sole legitimate model of family life was patriarchal, the black male was marginalized as a father and husband, so that the whole society, white and black, could be subjected to the domination of the white master class. But because black family ties were disrupted, this does not mean that they were not deeply felt. There is evidence of great attachment to family relations among slaves, precisely because this was the only bond slaves had autonomously. Great efforts were made by slaves to hold the family together or to contact scattered members.

This disrupted condition of the black family worsened in the postbellum South. Having destroyed slavery, which did afford a certain job security and feudal ties of responsibility, white society was unwilling to replace it with real socioeconomic integration. Jim Crow laws asserted a rigid racial caste system. Black women were still made available to white males on demand, but the ways of enforcing that were more hidden. The black male found himself not only deprived of social respect, but of any means of making a stable livelihood to support a family. Repressing its sexual guilt, white male society projected its pathology upon the black male. He became the walking symbol of white fears of retribution. He was fantasized into a dark sexual "beast," with outsized penis, ever about to assault the barricades that protected the white man's "virginal" female. Hundreds of black men, their genitals ripped from their bodies, were left to twist on trees as sacrificial victims of this obsession. Not surprisingly some black men themselves, denied other forms of respect, began to fancy themselves as the embodiments of the elemental male virility that white society had imagined them to be.[3]

Postbellum white racism was a system not only of economic and social deprivation of the black group, but also of the direct terrorization of the black family, directed especially against the black male. As a result it was often left to the black woman to support and even physically defend the black family. Black men fled, drifted, languished in prison, or ended violently. Nathan Hare, in an article entitled "The Frustrated Masculinity of the Negro Male," talks of the continued effects of this terrorization even within the civil rights movement. Often the first blows for social justice were struck by black women. It was they who first braved their way into schools and refused to sit down in the back of the bus.[4] For black men to assert themselves in the South was more dangerous.

But black women also played the ambiguous role of being the mother who felt the need to socialize her sons into patterns of docility and avoidance of confrontation, in order to minimize this terrorism. In this sense the black mother comes to be seen as "castrating" her son. Yet black women sometimes struck back directly in behalf of their humiliated sons and husbands. One story is told of an incident in which a young black male was struck in the face by a white plantation owner. When his mother was told of the incident, she took off down the path whence her son had fled home, thrashed the white man, and left him on the ground with his clothes torn from his back. The point of the story is that if the son had so retaliated he could have expected terrible retribution. The black woman could occasionally strike back because no white southern man would want to admit being beaten up by a black woman. Perhaps, too, he had to deal with the black mother as the "mammy" whose breasts also suckled him. Thus southern society created a complex interweaving of racism and sexism, blood guilt and blood ties, between whites and blacks. This left the black male humiliated not only in relation to white males, but in relation to his own family, his own wife and children, as well.[5]

Today this humiliated condition of the black man has greatly changed for growing numbers of black families. Its legacy survives in the disrupted patterns of the black lower class. But the memory of that terrorism still forms the ultimate point of reference for black liberation. This is why the dominant motif of the black movement has not been black feminism, but black masculinity. The black liberation movement has been overwhelmingly male oriented in its style and leadership.

WHITE FEMINISM AND BLACK LIBERATION

When white feminists meet the black movement, they are seldom aware of this history. They tend to be oblivious to the social encapsulation of their own analysis of sexism. They rebel against a "feminine mystique" that derives from the cult of the ornamental "white lady," unaware of the racist underpinnings of this image. They are hurt and alienated when the black movement, male and female, declares that this analysis of sexism is irrelevant to black people. Each side fails to see the way in which its experience of sexism and racism have been component parts of the total system of white patriarchal sexist-racism. We must see that the "white lady" is not only sexist but racist. It was in the name of this cult that black women were sexually debased and black men terrorized and even castrated.

It seems to me impossible for the black movement to respond to the sort of feminist theology represented by Mary Daly's recent book, *Beyond God the Father*, for example. The liberation symbols of this book are mostly mariological. Virginity, immaculate conception, and the assumption are held up as the symbols of feminine superiority. The judgmental symbol, on the other hand, is that of castration.[6] For black society, both of these symbols are totally encapsulated in white racism, through which both black women and black men have been victimized. Far from being liberating, such symbols seem simply expressions of white sexual pathology conducting business as usual.

When we look at the history of white feminism in America, we see that the fears of the black movement that a feminism defined by elite white women will be not only irrelevant, but antithetical to black liberation have some basis. White women tend to remember that the women's movement arose in the 1830s as an integral part of the antislavery movement. The first feminists were abolitionists, whose consciousness about sexism was raised when male clergy and colleagues refused to let them speak. Similarly the second women's movement in the 1960s arose through the radicalization of women working against racism and war in the civil rights and peace movements. Thus the women's movement perceives itself to have always espoused solidarity with the black movement, and to be unjustly refused reciprocal solidarity. But this is a partial truth.

At the end of the Civil War the Fourteenth Amendment, which enfranchised the Negro, explicitly excluded women, using the word *male* as a qualification for citizenship for the first time in American constitutional history. The more militant leaders of the women's movement were furious and opposed the amendment until it would include both race and sex. This separation of race and sex was the work of white male legislators, although Frederick Douglass did urge the women to "let the Freedman have his day," and to work for the enfranchisement of women as a second step. But the alienation of the women's movement from the cause of black liberation began at that point and increasingly drifted toward a racist and class bias.

As the women's movement became a mass movement in the 1880s, it was influenced by the general abandonment of libertarianism for a racist social Darwinism. Even the Social Gospel movement, which preached against the exploitation of labor, acquiesced to the leading scientific dogma of Negro racial inferiority. Moreover, it remained paternalistic in its basic concept of reform, seeing this primarily as the acculturation of the immigrant class into the superior ways of WASP puritanism. The women's movement drifted toward a rationale for the enfranchisement of women that restricted this to white upper-class women. It simultaneously acquiesced in the disfranchisement of the Negro and the immigrant in Jim Crow and literacy laws. It thus revealed the essential danger of a women's movement, namely, that it can be diverted into a crusade on the side of the status quo, and become a means by which the ruling class doubles the power and votes of its own class and racial group, while excluding lower classes and oppressed races. The point was made succinctly by a resolution passed at the national women's suffrage convention in 1893:

> *Resolved:* that without expressing any opinion on the proper qualification for voting, we call attention to the significant facts that in every state there are more women that can read and write than all the negro voters; more white women who can read and write than all the negro voters; more American women who can read and write than all the foreign voters, so that the enfranchisement of such women would settle the vexed question of rule by illiteracy, whether of homegrown or foreign-born production.[7]

The point was made in far more ringing terms by Belle Kearney of Mississippi at the 1903 convention, which sealed the pact of women's suffrage and white supremacy:

> Some day the North will be compelled to look to the South for redemption from these evils, on account of the purity of its Anglo-Saxon blood, the simplicity of its social and economic structure, the great advance made in prohibitory law and the maintenance of the sanctity of its faith, which has been kept inviolate. Just as surely as the North will be forced to turn to the South for the nation's salvation, just so surely will the South be compelled to look to its Anglo-Saxon women as the medium through which to retain the supremacy of the white race over the African. . . . Anglo-Saxonism is the standard of the ages to come. It is, above all, the granite foundation of the South. Upon that its civilization will mount; upon that it will stand unshaken.[8]

In addition to this capitulation toward an advocacy of women's suffrage as the consolidation of the power of the WASP ruling class, the women's movement backed away from any confrontation with the stereotypes of masculinity and femininity and the role of women in the home. Instead it attempted to grasp the doctrine of women's greater moral purity and nurturing nature to argue for their role in the public sphere as guardian of traditional morals. The conservatives used the same views of women to argue that they must remain segregated in the home, as the only sure safeguard of their purer and more moral "natures." The anticlimactic result of the final victory of women's suffrage must be explained in part by the weapons which the later suffrage movement consented to use, although it is doubtful that any other weapons would have won them this victory in an America in the throes of racist and class backlash on every side.

It would seem that the women's movement today is little disposed to fall into these traps again. The ideology of racism is much more consciously rejected among women radicals. The women's movement has centered its attack upon the stereotypes of the feminine mystique, and the role of women in the home. Yet it seems to me the tendency in radical feminism to make an exclusivistic analysis of sexism, and to refuse to recognize the interstructuring of sexism with class and racism, may tend to work a similar sort of social encapsulation. This means that, to a large extent, the analysis of sexism remains confined to the experience of a fairly atypical group of white, usually childless women, who belong, racially and socioeconomically, to the ruling class.

There is little recognition of the class and race-bound nature of the roles and symbols which they attack. The white woman who complains of sexual repression and ornamental leisure has little consciousness of the reverse experience of the black woman, at whose expense this mystique and leisure have been purchased. They are even less aware that not all males in our society rule the roost, but some are humiliated and marginalized in their own homes by these same forces. These myopias make the women's movement oblivious to the ways in which its own demands for rights are actually demands for the class and race privileges of their brothers and fathers. To decry the lack of female tenured professors at Harvard is far away from the concerns of poor black women, who are at the bottom of a society divided not only by sex, but by class and race as well. A monolithic analysis of sexism as the ultimate oppression obscures the way in which sexism is structurally integrated with class and race.

Sociologically, women are a caste within every class and race. They share a common condition of women in general: dependency, secondary existence, domestic labor, sexual exploitation, and the projection of their role in procreation into a total definition of their existence. But this common condition takes profoundly different forms, as women are divided against each other by class and race. In a real sense, any women's movement which is *only* concerned about sexism and no other form of oppression, must remain a women's movement of the white upper class, for it is *only* this group of women whose *only* problem is the problem of being women, since, in every other way, they belong to the ruling class. But a woman who belongs to other minority groups must inevitably refuse this monolithic analysis. She must integrate her struggle as a woman into the struggle to liberate her racial and socioeconomic group. Thus it seems to me essential that the women's movement reach out and include in its struggle the interstructuring of sexism with all other kinds of oppression, and recognize a pluralism of women's movements in the context of different groupings. Otherwise it will tend to remain a women's movement of the ruling class that can be misused to consolidate the power of that ruling class against the poor and nonwhite of both sexes.

THE SEXISM OF THE BLACK (MALE) MOVEMENT

If the women's movement is endangered by class and race bias, there is no doubt that the black movement in America has a bias toward a compensatory male chauvinism. Both the black church and black nationalism are characterized by the drive to restore, often in exaggerated form, the prerogatives of humiliated black maleness, taking for granted the traditional patriarchal images of manhood. In the black underclass the male was humiliated as economic provider and protector of his family. But this hardly means that he became "castrated" or "effeminate" sexually, contrary to the stupid Freudianism floating around in studies such as the Moynihan Report. The "impotency" of the black male did not affect him sexually, but socioeconomically. This very concept of "impotency" reveals the way in which white society links manliness with socioeconomic power and status. Because of his failure in this arena, the black male often could look on marriage only as a place of conflict and humiliation. But he could compensate for this by super-*macho* behavior on the level of personality and sexual prowess.

The large number of young black males killed or imprisoned means that the black woman has a very disadvantageous sex ratio with black men. This is further aggravated when black men date white women, as they now are able to do. Thus, although the black woman might have the more stable income, this has seldom allowed her to call the tune in sexual relations. The black male became an elusive figure, often abandoning his family when ego failure became too much to bear. The black woman had to take her sexual companionship pretty much on male terms. She could expect little help with the child-raising or housework. To rebuke such a woman as a "castrating matriarch" is to fail to see the powerlessness which is the basis of her role. If she has an autonomy and a strength, it is the product of the hard school of poverty and abandonment. Her wages are the lowest of any group, including the black male. Her survival and ability to make her work the foundation of many a family should be a tribute, not an indictment. White society compounded her dilemma, for as soon as her man failed as economic provider, he was forced out of the home as father and companion because the condition for the reception of welfare payments was the removal of any adult male from the home.

The black church has traditionally been highly patriarchal and has served to integrate the black family symbolically into the Western patriarchal family norm. This is less true for Pentecostal and storefront churches which sometimes have reflected the pattern of female-run homes, being founded and run largely by women who are heads of families and band together to serve their own needs. In the context of this type of storefront church, it is not incongruous to think of the bishop or pastor as community grandmother.

But the mainline black churches have typically functioned to validate black male identity. The black church was the one institution publicly owned and run by the black community. It was the basis of training in politics and economic development. Therefore it was the center of a male public world of power and business in a way quite different from the white church, which is typically segregated in the feminine, suburban sector of white society. By contrast, the black minister becomes the original patriarch of the black community, a surrogate for the absent fathers of the black family. In a society where black maleness was castrated socioeconomically, the black church displayed the black father restored to his "rightful" place as head of the household. This compensatory role made the black minister a symbol of pride whom the whole community could endow with the potency and pride denied to themselves. But if the black church was where black manliness was restored to the Judeo-Christian norm, it was also the place where the black community emulated the Calvinist norm of converted or righteous behavior (contrary to the stereotypes of white society about blacks). The black church emulated the standards of hard work and puritanical attitudes toward sexuality as a way of dissociating itself from the black lower class.

Black nationalism breaks with some of these tendencies of the black church by seeking to bridge the gap between the "respectable" blacks and the disrupted conditions of the black lower class. Contrary to the pacified patterns of the black church, it appropriates the images of maleness of supersexuality and the "big gun." But in other ways Black nationalism continues the tendencies of the black church toward repatriarchalization and embourgeoisement of the black community. This is particularly evident in the Black Muslims. Here the male is regarded as the absolute dictator of the home, toward whom both women and children owe complete submission. The father's word is law. All employment of women outside the home is discouraged. Women and girls are clothed in long garments reminiscent of Islamic purdah, signaling their submission and property status in relationship to the male. Men are dressed in the severe, somber garb of the traditional black Calvinist church. All the puritan virtues of obedience, hard work, self-discipline, and abstinence from fleshly pleasures are inculcated. The role of women is that of domesticity and fertile motherhood.[9]

Why would any black women accept this reduction of her traditional spirit? For many black women, especially the poor of the urban ghettos, where the Muslims make the majority of their recruits, this docility may seem a price worth paying. The Muslim faith guarantees that she will receive in return a faithful and dutiful husband, who will not drink, be violent, "run around," or abandon his family, and will hold a steady job that returns an income on schedule. White feminists must measure the extreme patriarchalism of the Muslims against the worse conditions under which black women have been forced to live in American urban slums. Black Muslims are an extreme example of the triumph of puritan patriarchalism among the black lower class. But other black nationalist groups have shown some similar tendencies to demand the submission of the black woman to visible symbols of male dominance as the price of the new "black pride."

BLACK FEMINISM AND BLACK PRIDE

The black woman seems to be an immediate target of much of the masculinity complex of black pride. It is she whose autonomy and independent ways are to be curtailed by the exercise of black *machismo.* It is she who is called to "step back" so that "her man" can display himself as the fierce warrior, large machine-gun in hand, or as the successful provider of status and security for his family. Many black women are willing to make this trade, since its alternative has been poverty, abandonment, and a demoralized male population. But many black women are quietly seeking an alternative analysis. They are pointing out that black women have been the "reality principle" for black consciousness; they have been the foundation of black survival under oppression. This accomplishment should be regarded with pride as a part of black history.

The tradition of autonomy and strength in black women makes possible an alternative paradigm of black male-female relations. They need not be patterned after white patriarchy, but now can be reciprocal and mutually enhancing, as black men and women advance side by side in their accomplishments. There is an anxiety among black women to affirm their full solidarity with the enhancement of black "manhood." Only very carefully do a few suggest that black male status should not be measured by black female submission. A few outspoken voices point out that this is an adolescent and self-defeating form of manliness and that it fails to appreciate the potential alternatives for black male-female relations created by the experience of the black family under oppression.[10]

For obvious reasons, black women are very reticent to make this analysis openly and in the context of relations with white racist society. They shrink from any feminism that would divide them from solidarity with black communal liberation. Moreover they feel that the white middle-class-dominated women's movement does not express their experience. The black woman experiences the white woman as both a sexual rival and a person whose symbolic existence has been constantly exploited to oppress black women and to both terrorize and attract the black male. Thus there seems little that draws black women to immediate feelings of solidarity with white women. How many little black girls were allowed to cherish baby dolls with white skin and silky yellow hair and then were devastated when they realized their own distance from this reigning ideal of beauty? Economically, white women appeared as the proximate oppressors of black women. They were the pampered darlings, freed from their own mothering and household chores by black women, so they could cultivate the ornamental femininity prized by white males. Much bitter hostility fills the memories of black women toward white women, which makes it difficult for them to discover each other as common victims of white patriarchalism. (Needless to say, only a tiny minority of white women actually enjoy the "white lady" role.)

Black nationalism is placing black women at the crossroads of contradictory tendencies. It would be important to find out to what extent the rigid patriarchal and puritanical patterns which some black nationalists seem to wish to impose on black women really succeed in affecting large numbers of black women. It is unfortunate that the general lack of class analysis in the black left in America has prevented it from incorporating the Marxist feminist tradition which is found in third world liberation movements in China, Vietnam, and Cuba. Instead, the third world model drawn upon by black nationalists has come from an identification with Arab nationalism, with its unrevised traditions of total subordination of woman. In American urban centers one sees black women dressed in various kinds of flowing dress and veils, docilely trailing the Black male, with close-spaced children in tow. How widespread this pattern is, and what kind of repressed tensions this is creating in a society where black women were traditionally highly vocal and autonomous, is unknown.

On the other hand, many black middle-class families build on the traditional role of black women as economic providers in order to create a family pattern where it is normal for both husband and wife to be equally employed. From my experience in Washington, D.C., this black middle-class-family pattern seems much more common than in comparable white families. This pattern of dual professions is probably necessary if the black family is to gain sufficient income to attain middle-class status. There is a need for studies which pay particular attention to this changing status of the black woman in relation to the historical patterns of the black family in America.

The women's movement should certainly see itself as especially concerned with this topic. Yet this is a difficult task, because black women themselves must be the ones to take the initiative in an analysis of their needs. They have had little forum for doing this in the male-dominated black movement and little disposition for doing it in the white-dominated women's movement. A greater sensitivity is needed in the women's movement to the interstructuring of race, sex, and class, so that the differing experiences of particular groups of women can be acknowledged. Only as autonomous women's movements arise in the context of various kinds of race, ethnic, and class oppression will the missing links in the structure of oppression begin to become visible. Black feminism especially might throw new light on what has been involved in the formation of the male personality in sexist society, since black women have seen the effects of that personality formation, both in its pride and in its humiliation.

Finally we must recognize a certain psychological root to the tendency of both the black movement and the women's movement to ignore the structures of oppression within their own groups and to attempt to reduce "oppression" to a single-factored analysis. The Western apocalyptic model of liberation theology polarizes the world into "light" and "darkness," elect and damned, good and evil. Liberation movements draw on the same tendency to absolute polarity, but in a reverse form. To recognize structures of oppression within our own group would break up this model of ultimate righteousness and projection of guilt upon the "others." It would force us to deal with ourselves, not as simply oppressed or oppressors, but as people who are sometimes one and sometimes the other in different contexts. A more mature and chastened analysis of the capacities of human beings for good and evil would flow from this perception. The flood gates of righteous anger must then be tempered by critical self-knowledge. This is a blow to the ego of adolescent revolutionary personalities. But, in the long run, only this more complex self-knowledge gives us hope that liberation movements will not run merely to the reversal of hatreds and oppressions, but rather, to a recovery of a greater humanity for us all.

Notes

1. See R. W. Fogel and Stanley Engermann, *Time on the Cross: The Economics of American Negro Slavery* (Boston: Little, Brown, 1973), and *Time on the Cross: Evidence and Methods* (Boston: Little, Brown, 1973); also review by C. Vann Woodward, "The Jolly Institution," *The New York Review of Books*, May 2, 1974, pp. 3–6.

2. B. A. Botkin, *Lay My Burden Down* (Chicago: University of Chicago Press, 1945), quoted in Jessie Bernard, *Marriage and Family Among Negroes* (Englewood Cliffs, N.J.: Prentice-Hall, 1966), p. 9. See also Andrew Billingsley, *Black Families in White America* (Englewood Cliffs, N.J.: Prentice-Hall, 1968), pp. 48–71.

3. For the various myths and behavior pathologies of the four groups toward each other, see Calvin Hernton, *Sexism and Racism in America* (Garden City, N.J.: Doubleday, 1965).

4. This point was made by Nathan Hare, "The Frustrated Masculinity of the Negro Male," *Negro Digest*, August 1964, pp. 5–9; reprinted in Robert Staples, *The Black Family: Essays and Studies* (Belmont, Calif.: Wadsworth Publishing Co., 1971), pp. 131–34. See also the issue on the Black Male, *The Black Scholar*, 2, No. 10 (June 1971).

5. Robert Staples, "The Myth of the Black Matriarchy," *The Black Scholar*, January-February 1970), pp. 8–16; reprinted in *The Black Family*, pp. 149–59.

6. Daly, *Beyond God the Father* (Boston:: Beacon Press, 1973), pp. 19, 82–92.

7. *NAWSA Proceedings*, 1893, p. 84; quoted in Aileen Kraditor, *The Ideas of the Women's Suffrage Movement, 1890–1920* (Garden City, N.Y.: Doubleday, 1965), p. 110.

8. *Woman's Journal*, April 4, 1903; quoted in Aileen Kraditor, *op. cit.*, pp. 160–1.

9. Harry Edwards, "Black Muslim and Negro Christian Family Relationships," *Journal of Marriage and the Family*, 30 (November 1968), pp. 604–11; reprinted in Robert Staples, *The Black Family*, pp. 376–87.

10. See various articles in the anthology by Toni Cade, *The Black Woman* (New York: Signet Books, 1970).

PART THREE

Women: The Last Revolution

The Psychoanalytic Revolution: Friend or Enemy of Women?

THE PSYCHOANALYTIC REVOLUTION IS ONE OF THE MOST important changes in consciousness which separates us from our forebears of even a century ago, who could still regard their consciousness as a direct reflection of "reality." Psychoanalytic thought has made us recognize the enormous amount of self-deceit and false perception of others involved in ordinary consciousness. Freud's discovery of the processes of repression and projection are enormously important for understanding the dynamics of sexism. Marxism can reveal the way in which the ideologies of sexism rationalize the enslavement of women in the roles of reproducer, unpaid domestic servant, and surplus laborer. But the irrational dimension of sexism and the denial of individuation to women in order to make them the bearers of the suppressed wishes and fears of the dominant males are insights which demanded the psychoanalytic revolution of consciousness. Psychoanalysis is an important tool which women's liberation must itself liberate in order to use it to analyze the historic denigration of women and also to create the therapeutic side of the process of liberation, to guide them to psychic health, past the shoals of resentment and despair. It is therefore one of the great tragedies of our times that the potential of psychoanalysis has been perverted so drastically precisely in relation to women. Its theorists seem to have been keen-sighted toward every form of false consciousness except this one. Psychoanalysis has become the chief tool, replacing patriarchal religion, for rationalizing and sanctifying the inferiority of women. Women can lay hold of psychoanalytic techniques only through a thoroughgoing critique of the sexist perversion of psychoanalytic theory.

FREUD AND "FEMININITY"

Freud, the discoverer of the importance of repressed sexuality, was also the founder of the sexist perversion of psychoanalytic interpretation. This fact must give one pause about the whole structure of his thought. How could this have happened? Freud accepted the classical scholastic view that women are biologically defective and that this limits and conditions the entire course of their psychological development, barring them from the higher realms of intelligence and moral discipline. For Freud, male genital characteristics are the normative foundation of full humanity, in relation to which women are defined as deprived or "castrated." The peculiarity of this view can be readily seen if we turn it around. Suppose one were to say that the male was fundamentally incapable of developing interiority or spiritual depth because he lacks a womb. Even Erik Erikson, with his exaltation of woman's "inner space," does not go that far.[1] But Freud took the woman's lack of a penis literally as an ontological defect, fundamentally limiting her ability to develop into an autonomous, rational person.

And yet, oddly enough, Freud believes that infant boys and girls start out much alike. Both have the same kind of libidinal drives. Libido is bisexual, or identical in boys and girls. Yet, at other times, he speaks of it as essentially male, assuming that women have a share in masculine libido. This is a striking example of his conflation of the generic with the masculine. Freud's description of the development of girls from this bisexual beginning-point goes like this.[2] Both boy and girl infants have the same desire to love and possess the mother. This is based on the infant's libidinal attachment to the mother as the source of life and nourishment. This oral attachment to the mother somehow moves toward a desire to possess the mother, which Freud speaks about as though it were genital or incestuous. However, early in childhood, girls make a traumatic discovery which, ever after, conditions their psychic development. They discover that they lack a penis. They lack the organ to possess the mother. The girl-child's self-esteem suffers a devastating blow, as she compares her genitals with those of her brother. She blames her mother for depriving her of the necessary equipment.

The girl turns away from the mother to the more powerful father in hopes of receiving a penis, which he has and her mother lacks. Her psychic development thereafter is a frustrated quest to receive from males, either the father, a husband, or a son, the potency which she has been deprived of by nature. This quest can lead women toward three possible types of psychological development.[3] They can withdraw into neurosis or resentment, burying feelings of deprivation in a refusal to relate to others at all. Or, second, they can refuse to accept the fact of their castrated natures and organize themselves around their rudimentary penis or clitoris, which gave them pleasure and was the basis of their oedipal desires as an infant. This Freud calls the "masculinity complex." Such women try to emulate men and to pretend that they have exactly the same natures as men. Freud regarded the "aggressive," professional woman or the woman intellectual as this kind of "infantile," clitoral woman, who has refused to accept her castrated nature. Freud interpreted even the entrance of women into psychoanalysis as an expression of penis-envy, whereby the frustrated female seeks to get from the psychoanalyst-father what her own father had failed to give her. Significantly, Freud attracted many women patients. Also the early psychoanalytical circle contained a number of unusually brilliant women disciples. These facts lend an odd ring to

Freud's view of the woman intellectual, and the woman interested in psychoanalysis, as a woman driven by penis-envy, whose libido remains fixated at the infantile, clitoral stage.

In contrast to these neurotic or immature paths of development, Freud described what he called "normal femininity." This third type is the woman who gradually comes to accept her biological fate and resigns herself to her secondary and dependent destiny. This demands a shift of the seat of her desires from the rudimentary, active libido in the clitoris to the vagina, where she awaits penetration by the male as the source of her feminine fulfillment. Only by giving up her masculinity-drive and shifting the form of her libido to that appropriate to her true biological destiny, namely, as a passive, dependent orifice that waits upon masculine activity for her needs, do women finally receive the compensation for their deprivation, i.e., a baby. Of course, not just any baby will do. What women desire primarily is a boy-baby —the "penis-baby" through which they possess, vicariously in their son, what they have been deprived of in themselves. To produce a girl-baby is to create just another mutilation. At this point, according to Freud's theory, the secondary character of the female becomes inherited through the mother herself, who must begin her own daughter's life by reacting to it with disappointment. Only a son can satisfy the frustrated desire of the woman for fulfillment. Women's normative psychic development is to give up autonomy and initiative and shape themselves to live as passive, dependent vessels of male activity and vicarious appendages of male offspring. One might say that what Freud has described is the "making of a Jewish mother," although, of course, Freud's own ethnic background only gave especially forceful form to the basic mandate which patriarchal culture as a whole places upon women.

It is important to see that, for Freud, the female castration-trauma is fundamentally different from the male castration-fear. The boy-child desires to possess the mother, and he encounters the father as a threatening force who can punish him for this illicit desire. The boy turns from the mother to the father as an act of repression of this guilty desire and a recognition of his inability, at this stage, to compete with the superior penis of the father. Yet the boy learns by this attachment to law, represented by the father, the instinctual control for moral discipline and the sublimation of the libido necessary for the works of intellect and higher culture.

The female castration-trauma, on the other hand, is not the repression of a guilty desire, but the discovery of a fundamental truth. The boy fears to lose the potency which he has and so learns to control it until he is able to actualize it fully. The female discovers that she is fundamentally deprived of this potency by nature. Thus, according to Freud, the girl's turn to the father is not an act of self-discipline, but an act of frustrated hope. Women therefore never achieve the instinctual sublimation that comes to the male through his need to repress his desires. Theirs is an empty élan, based on deprivation, which must crash and turn back upon itself. Women, therefore, remain fixated at a narcissistic and masochistic level of psychic development and are "little able to manage the instinctual repressions necessary for intelligence, moral discipline and higher culture." [4] Women, according to Freud, remain alien to and resentful of culture, which takes men away from them into the larger world of thought and activity. Even the masculine or clitoral woman does not fully manage a mature superego, for her psychology remains motivated by envy and frustration. The intelligence of intelligent women, therefore, remains characterized by a hollow and spiteful tone that demonstrates its lack of real foundation.

THE POST-FREUDIAN CRITIQUE OF
FREUDIAN SEXISM

The Freudian circle itself early began to feel some inade-
quacy in this definition of female psychology. Even Freud
expressed various doubts about his ability to understand
the data, and, late in life, admitted that he didn't know
"What it was that women wanted." [5] Helene Deutsch is
usually thought to be the most faithful of Freud's female
disciples in repeating this orthdox viewpoint, and her
own biography suggests that she found Freud's analysis
accurate in her own attachment, first to her father, and
then to Freud himself. Yet a careful reading of her work
suggests that she subtlely transmuted the content of
Feud's definition of female psychology as one dominated
by masochism, narcissism, and passivity. She dis-
counted the importance of the castration-trauma, and
transformed these characteristics from negative to positive qualities, where they become descriptive of the
woman's essential "feminine core" of interiority, inner
strength, and the power to bear and to nurture others.[6]

Others in the Freudian circle went further in their criti-
cisms. Alfred Adler turned away from the libidinal to the
power drive as the most important organizing energy of
psychic development. From this point of view he discerned that what might be called "penis-envy" in women
does not reflect an ontological deficiency, but an envy of
male power. He regarded the entire psychodynamics of
both male and female psychic development as fundamentally distorted because of male domination. What is
called "masculine" is the egoistic attitudes of the powerful, and what is derogated is "feminine" is the defeated
traits of the powerless, both of which have little to do
with the full potential of men and women as they might
exist in an equalitarian society. The penis does not give
men biological superiority over women, but is the symbol
of their social domination over women.[7]

Karen Horney, who broke with Freud over her rejection of the orthodox Freudian definition of women, attempted a thoroughgoing redefinition of the theory. In an early essay she showed that Freud's definition of women is, in fact, a rationalized version of every little boy's view of girls, which has been projected upon girls and presumed to reflect little girls' feelings and experiences of themselves. If it were true that little girls do experience themselves in this way, what it reflects is a social power of the male image in society so overwhelming that it has succeeded, even at so early an age, at burying the little girl's experience of her own body as normative for herself, substituting instead the male body as normative (as the basis of social power) in relation to which the girl feels deprived.[8]

But Horney went further than exposing the projection mechanisms of the idea of "penis-envy." She also attempted to reconstruct the mechanisms of male misogynism which underlie these rationalizations of female inferiority. Buried under these rationalizations there exists in male experience a primary reaction to women as beings who appear more autonomous and more central to the generative processes than males. This is the image of women that appeared in early mother-centered cultures, but reappears in every generation. Men experience themselves as more marginal to the business of procreation than women. Moreover, women transmute a part of their generative energy into procreation, becoming autonomous or self-fulfilled, leaving the male somewhat out in the cold. The mother-child circle replaces the circle of lovers. The mother, absorbed in the pleasure of producing and feeding the child, has little sexual interest in the male. The male feels his marginality, his dependence for his own pleasure on the woman who, for large periods of time, neither wants nor needs him for her libidinal gratification, which becomes concentrated on her own creation.

The male castration complex also reflects this initial male experience of the power and primacy of the female. In copulation the male must entrust his genitals to the woman and "lose" a part of himself. The sexual act leaves the male feeling depleted, with a sense of having lost his potency to the woman who takes it to herself and uses it. The pervasive sexual taboos, which have arisen in classical religious systems, that regard the retention of semen as a way of retaining male potency, and the avoidance of women as a way of building up strength, either for war or for sports, or sublimated as spiritual strength—such ideas reflect, often in elaborate ascetic, mystical systems, this primary male experience. Much of the effort of males to subordinate women and make them become passive, dependent, and auxiliary to the male must be seen as male revenge: an effort to use the relative muscular superiority of the male to compensate for and overwhelm these original feelings of being ontologically dependent and auxiliary to the female in the sexual and generative processes.[9] All the myths of female inferiority, from Adam's rib to Freud himself, then must be seen as a male suppression of this primary intuition of female primacy and potency and an attempt to create power relations between the sexes so that the potent, autonomous mother goddess is transformed into the passive, secondary, daughter-bride, Eve, totally dependent on the male for her *raison d'être*. (In this connection one might also ask whether the Freudian concept of the Oedipal experience is really the child's experience so much as an attitude originating in the father's envy of the exclusivity of the mother-child relationship.)

More recent biological discoveries have added new ammunition to this uncovering of the male ideological character of Freud's theories. Although Freud recognized that the clitoris is the biological analogue of the penis in women, he insisted that women who remain attached to their clitoris as the seat of libidinal pleasure remain "infantile." Oddly enough, to remain clitoral is also the route to aggressivity, autonomy, and intellectuality for women, which leads Freud to define autonomous, intellectual women as "infantile". Maturity for women consists in giving up the autonomous seat of pleasure in the clitoris for the passive "vaginal orgasm." Only in this way can women become feminine and fulfilled, i.e., wives and mothers.

The research on female sexuality by Masters and Johnson has exploded this concept that women have two different kinds of orgasm, as well as the Victorian perception of the woman as having a lesser capacity for erotic pleasure than males.[10] They discovered that the vagina itself has no erotic sensitivity, and all orgasm for women is based on the stimulation of the clitoris. To insist on a norm of sexuality for women without clitoral stimulation, and defined by male penetration, is a sexuality defined by male eroticism which leaves women feeling sexually unsatisfied. Women are structured into passive vessels of male sexuality and generation, and are left with the impression that they themselves have little capacity for erotic feeling. Freud's concept of the shift to the vaginal orgasm, then, not only promotes the making of the Jewish mother, but also the making of the Victorian lady, who is supposed to have little capacity for sexual feeling of her own, and to see herself as the passive vehicle of male sexuality. Masters and Johnson demonstrated that, properly stimulated, women have a capacity for multiple orgasms, in contrast to the male, whose orgasmic experience is more of a "one-shot" affair. Freud's doctrine of the vaginal orgasm turns out to be one of those great examples of false biology, similar to Aristotle's definition of women as misbegotten males who contribute nothing to the formation of the fetus, i.e., denial of the female ovum. The autonomous nature of female sexuality is denied in a male biologistic ideology in order to define women as auxiliaries of an entirely male-centered activity.

The embryological research popularized in the writings of Mary Jane Sherfey has further exposed these links between Freudian and Aristotelian false biology. Sherfey has shown that modern embryology has come to recognize that the human fetus is originally female. That is to say, the embryo contains the organs of both males and females in the female form. The biological male is developed in the uterus through a differentiation out of the original female form. Biologically speaking, it is more correct to define the penis as an overgrown clitoris, than to regard the clitoris as a residual penis. This process by which the male develops by a differentiation out of the female is necessary in mammals, where both sexes develop in the female ambit of the mother's womb. The opposite process would take place in species where the eggs are fertilized and grow extra-uterinely, i.e., in snakes. Sherfey, however, shows that this understanding is often elaborately mystified in biological texts because, in male-dominated societies, the myth of the primacy of the male, from which the female is developed (Adam's rib, again) rationalizes the social identification of the male with generic humanity, in relation to which women are seen as secondary and auxiliary.[11]

The Freudian definition of women thus turns out to be, in many ways, the psychoanalytic analogue of the religious myth of Eve as Adam's rib. It is not surprising, therefore, that Freudian psychoanalysts early began to concern themselves with trying to entangle the meaning of this myth. Freud himself recognized that there was something peculiar about this story. Otto Rank proposed what was to become the orthodox Freudian explanation of it by suggesting that it really conceals the Oedipus incest story. The real meaning is the reverse of the overt story, concealing the desire of the infant to marry the mother. Eve is really Adam's mother.

Theodore Reik, in his essay *The Making of Woman*, recounts his own exploration of the meaning of this story. He felt unsatisfied with Rank's explanation. He tells of his intuition, even as a young child, that the meaning of the story must lie in its reversal. He grew up in a Jewish family divided by the conflict between his father's generation, which had become secular and scientific, and his grandfather's generation, which still belonged to the traditional religious culture. His grandfather, hoping to influence the child, allowed him to sit in on the discussions of rabbinic exegesis that took place among a circle of old men. Whenever a particularly puzzling problem came up which could not be solved any other way, one rabbinic technique was to apply the principle of *tomer verkerht*, i.e., "perhaps the real meaning lies in turning the terms around." One day the old man and his friends were puzzling over the story of Eve's birth and making little sense out of it. Through some unknown inspiration the little boy suddenly shouted out, *Tomer verkerht*! To his surprise the elderly Jewish men arose in a rage and threw the boy out of their midst, never again allowing him to listen in on their discussions.

Reik himself comes to the conclusion that the story is one that has evolved over a long period of time, concealing several layers of development. The earlier Genesis story would indeed have shown the male as born from the primal mother goddess. But the Eve story has been developed to repress this original Genesis story. This reflects the male puberty rite whereby the boy, in order to achieve manhood, must deny his original birth from the woman and be reborn from paternal power. But this should give us the story of a boy's birth from the father (i.e., the Father who begets the Son in the Christian Trinity). The story of a woman born from the male reflects yet a third stage, which incorporates the earlier stages of the repression of the mother goddess and the rebirth of the boy from the father, and moving on to the reappropriation of the woman as wife, but now in a subordinate, dependent relationship to the male. This is the final culmination of the rites of passage to manhood symbolized by the Eve story.[12]

From a feminist perspective, we can say that Reik

comes close to recognizing the creation-of-Eve story for what it is, namely, male ideology which seeks to deny the original experience of dependency on the matrix of nature, and on the mother, as both one's personal origin and the symbol of the primal matrix. Male culture seeks to reverse this relationship, so the male ego can see itself as supernatural or transcendent to nature, the creator of "the world" and of woman. Unfortunately Reik's study, like most psychoanalytic explorations of myth, never recognizes the patriarchal, social context of this myth. He therefore can take it as the norm for male psychological development, which must repress the image of the woman as creatrix, in order to recreate her as the secondary, dependent tool of male needs. Culturally speaking, women in patriarchal societies *are* Eve, in the sense that their original primacy has been repressed and they have been shaped and conditioned to appear as auxiliary beings of generic maleness. Women in patriarchal societies do not exist as themselves, but as cultural and ideological creations of male domination. Nothing can be said that is authentic to woman herself in patriarchal culture. This is as true of patriarchal psychoanalysis, sociology, economics, and anthropological sciences as it is of classical patriarchal religions and philosophies.

It seems then that the question in the title of this chapter must be answered in the negative. Freud's psychoanalytic revolution has been the enemy, not the friend, of women. Yet the psychoanalytical discovery of repression and projection is too important a tool for revealing the processes of male sexism itself to be simply rejected by women because it was originally shaped within a male ideological description of experience. Rather, feminists should judge Freud's account of the making of the "feminine woman" in a double way. We can say that this description is phenomenologically correct, as an analysis of what patriarchy must do to women in order to shape them to become what they are supposed to be, according to male definitions. Freud is an accurate observer of phenomena. His mistake lies in confusing social phenomena with "nature," both biologically and normatively. His description of how one frustrates a woman's original sense of her own potency, how one gradually convinces her to give up her élan toward individuation and autonomous self-expression, labeling her very strength as weakness, her drives toward what would be regarded as maturity, if applied to a male, as "infantile," so that she finally is convinced to collapse as a self-initiating human being and become a tool of male power—all this accurately describes what goes on in the making of the "normative female" in male-dominated societies.

To understand what Freud has done, one might make a racist analogy (since patriarchal society can still understand any other social problem better than sexism). Suppose some southern slaveowners had brought Freud several of their house servants to analyze for their psychological dysfunctions. Freud might accurately discern that these people were characterized by a contradiction between an externalized docility and an internalized rage that they must conceal, not only from the master, but from themselves, in order to conform to their social role, a rage which, however, tended to explode in neurotic symptoms.

Freud would trace back the psychological stages by which one takes a normally intelligent and expansive Negro child and shapes this child into a psychological "nigger." Taking the social role of the house slave as normative, Freud would then rationalize this inferiority as based on the biological inferiority of black skin and a dysfunctional "white-skin envy." He would prescribe a form of therapy designed to reinforce the process of nigger-making in order to obliterate, as much as possible, all consciousness of internal rage and to obtain, in the slave, a total resignation to this social role which is his "destiny."

Freud's description of the making of woman is analogous to this "nigger-making." He has accurately observed the processes by which patriarchal culture, within the family, strips the female sibling of her original sense of her autonomous, self-initiating personhood, and, in contrast with her brother, collapses her back into the destiny of her mother within the social system of male domination. But he has then rationalized this social process as based on female biological nature, and then suggested a therapy for women who have unsuccessfully managed this self-collapse that is designed to reinforce the process of self-collapse itself. This road to "maturity" for women is an antidevelopment, which would be immaturity for normal persons (males), while the desire for a personhood analogous to normative persons (males) is described, for women, as "infantile." Those who successfully repress their personhood, so they no longer feel any distress, are mature and normal "feminine" females. Those who are still distressed with a sense of the contradiction between their internal desires for personhood and their social destiny get a second chance to reinforce this original conditioning through Freudian therapy. If that fails, and they still feel an acute contradiction between their inner selves and their outer social mandate, they can become the casualties which fill our insane asylums. As Phyllis Chesler has pointed out, in her study of *Women and Madness*, the definition of women in patriarchal society, reinforced by orthodox psychotherapy, is basically a prescription for insanity for women.[13]

While Freud's biologistic and normative rationalizations of this process are totally vicious, what is highly useful for feminists is the accuracy of his description itself, considered as a psychosocial reflection of male domination. Juliet Mitchell, in her recent book *Psychoanalysis and Feminism*, has sought to rehabilitate Freud for feminists as highly accurate (even more so than later corrections, such as Reich and Laing).[14] However, Mitchell's effort to apologize for Freud's analysis as only phenomenological, and without biological or normative implications, seems to me inaccurate. It is true, Freud wishes to be a pure scientist and so often expresses doubts about the strict biological basis and normative character of his observations. Yet there is no doubt that he assumed penis-envy to be based on actual biological inferiority and proceeded to prescribe a therapy that took this description as the proper course of "normal" development for women, in relation to which either distress or rejection of male superiority was condemned as deviant behavior. Freud's orthodox followers may have made the relation between phenomena, biological foundation, and therapeutic prescription more rigid than Freud, but they were following the dominant tendency of the master in so doing. To be sure, Freud's description remains useful for feminists, despite these mistakes, once it is recognized for what it is. But the subsequent use of Freudianism as the chief tool for reinforcing patriarchal culture can hardly be understood unless it is recognized that the reification of this description as women's "nature," biologically and normatively, did originate with Freud himself.

"THE FEMININE" IN THE JUNGIAN TRADITION

Having spent considerable time on the Freudian tradition, I would like to turn briefly to a comparison of it with the Jungian tradition. Jung is often presumed to have a more positive concept of femininity, in contrast to Freud. In fact, however, both are exponents of nineteenth-century patriarchal doctrines of women. Freud represents the German misogynist tradition, which found extreme expression in Nietzsche and Schopenhauer, who attacked the liberated, intellectual woman as a threatening deviation. Women are regarded by "nature" as intellectually and morally inferior. They are "happy" only when they give up these "unnatural" demands for intellectuality and autonomy, and resign themselves to that sphere of bodily "nature" acted upon by an exclusively male capacity for culture.[15] Jung, on the other hand, represents the romantic tradition, which identifies woman with a more positive and mystical concept of "nature" as the unconscious, intuitive, spiritual depths of creative power. Jung also represents the mariological concept of the "spiritual feminine," in contrast to the identification of women with sensual bodiliness. Both views are equally disastrous to women's liberation. But the Jungian view is, in some ways, more dangerous because it is more seductive and its ideological character is not so readily apparent.

However, there are some aspects of the Jungian tradition which may be a positive correction to Freud. Jungians have a more positive view of the unconscious as a source of creative power and insight, the psychic matrix within which the consciousness is born and from which it needs to draw constantly for its power. Freud, on the other hand, tended to preserve the traditional rationalist model of the self, which views the unconscious as a cauldron of unruly appetites to be mastered by consciousness. Jung also believed that the ego or the persona is a superficial identity. We must draw upon the deeper, repressed side of ourself in the unconscious, both the "shadow" self and the sexual counterself that represents our psychic bisexuality, in order to reach mature personhood, or what Jung called "individuation." Jung also has a greater appreciation of specifically adult levels of psychic development. He sees full maturity as the birth of the androgynous self, which has integrated its repressed sides. This is a process that he sees going on in mature adulthood (thirty-five to fifty years old), beyond the ego identity shaped in early adulthood. Freud, by contrast, often gives us the impression that it is all over after early childhood, everything thereafter being simply the straightening out of what went wrong in the nursery.

Since Jung identifies the feminine with this deeper matrix of the unconscious, from which the fully mature self must be born, this leads him to a more positive appreciation of the feminine. The feminine symbols are not just the passive or negative sides of male rationality. They represent the more deeply creative side of "man," the source both of "his" original psychic birth and of "his" continual rebirth to higher states of consciousness (as we shall see, the male generic is appropriate here for Jung). Jung rejects the Freudian view of the Oedipal story, as an infantile desire for genital conquest of the mother. Rather, he sees the baby love for the mother as pregenital, a desire for fusion with the mother in order to recover the primal sense of unity and bliss that preceded the shock of birth. This primordial bliss and unity of the self with its maternal matrix is the source of the religious images of paradise. The desire to re-enter the mother is not merely regressive. It is also a positive élan through the stages of ego development and cultural growth until the differentiated self can finally transcend its separate and polarized self-definition to enter the higher unity symbolized by heaven and the new Jerusalem.

Here again the maternal symbol reappears, not just as the source of original life, but as the final goal of spiritual development. Here the woman appears as the eschatological feminine, the divine Sophia or Holy Wisdom, where self and community, humanity and nature, human and divine reunite in ultimate redemption. Jung, therefore, has a more positive appreciation of the uroboric stage of human development and the mother-centered symbols found in prepatriarchal cultures, symbols which reappear in the pregenital or bisexual stage of human development even within the patriarchal family. Freud also recognized the existence of this pre-Oedipal stage in the child, and the prepatriarchal stage in culture. But it remained a shadowy preamble to true civilization, which he assumed must necessarily be carried out exclusively under the sign of the Father. Any return to these symbols is regressive. Jung, by contrast, reappropriates this stage, so that it becomes the basis for continual development and, finally, for ultimate fulfillment.[16]

Erich Neumann's books *The Great Mother* and *The Origins and History of Consciousness* are the most ambitious effort in the Jungian tradition to lay out the correlation between stages of development in the individual psyche and the history of consciousness in culture expressed in the progress of mythopoetic symbols.[17] Much of Neumann's work aims at giving the matriarchal stage of culture its due as the original and ultimate matrix within which the ego develops. Neumann believes that the original genesis story was uroboric. The original foundation of reality is the primal egg or maternal womb, which contains its own self-fertilizing power. Out of this primal egg or uroboric mother there emerges the sky father and earth mother, not as a hierarchical relation, but as the differentiating out of complementary powers within the primal matrix. The ego begins to develop within early civilization in a way that is still under the dominion of the maternal symbol. The Great Mother of early mother-and-nature religion stands for Mother Nature, but as representative of the primal matrix. The god-king of early civilization reigns, but reigns from the lap of the Great Mother.

Patriarchal culture is then carried out as a struggle against this dominance of the ego by the Great Mother. Now the Mother becomes a negative threatening symbol, standing for the power of Nature to swallow up the finite ego back into her womb. The Great Mother becomes a symbol of the dragon and death, because, as the womb of birth, she is also the tomb into which the finite self returns. The ego seeks to establish itself as transcendent to and independent of the nature mother. In so doing the ego must posit a higher Father, a transcendent spirit father beyond the phallic father of the earlier nature religion. The hero becomes twice-born, reborn from the supernatural Father, thereby transcending the sphere of birth-and-death. Phallic masculinity must be sublimated, so that now it appears as intellect or spirit. The hero no longer fears castration so much as "blindness," the obliteration of the newly discovered spiritual powers by the threatening force of bodily nature "below." The cultural élan of the hero is defined by the "dragon fight," the struggle to defeat the nature mother and to define the ego as transcendent and autonomous to nature.

In this struggle a new feminine image appears beyond the Great Mother. This is the virgin goddess or anima sister, who must be rescued from the Great Mother to become a soul companion of the hero. The maiden rescued from the tower represents the feminine, no longer as nature mother, but as soul companion, not only fitted to be the spiritual friend of the hero, but even "his" inspirer and muse. The virgin goddess appears both beside and beyond the hero, helping him in his dragon fight and inspiring him to discover the creative powers of his soul. Here the woman appears as Athena, the virgin goddess who helps the hero in Homeric poetry, as the muse of the poets, the Lady Philosophia of philosophy, and the Virgin Mary of Christian asceticism. Finally, as the hero completes "his" journey, the Woman appears in her ultimate form as the new Jerusalem or Sophia, the ultimate Matrix which reunites the separated ego with the matrix of a spiritual or "new" creation, the reintegration of "nature" and "spirit."

Tantalizing as this description may be, nevertheless feminists must uncover its patriarchal, ideological character. Neumann has given us a fairly accurate description of the progress of symbols from within Western patriarchal culture of the Hellenistic-biblical variety, as it appropriates its earlier prepatriarchal roots in Near Eastern cultures. But, even within this framework, it must distort the actual content of certain key symbols in order to fit them into the patriarchal definition of the role of the "feminine." For example, the Great Mother is defined primarily as the sphere of "nature" in the sense of physical birth. The actual symbols of the Great Mother in ancient Near Eastern religions symbolized her not only as the source of natural fecundity, but also of law as well. She was not only the nature mother, but already the Queen of Heaven. Prepatriarchal religion united the symbols of heaven and earth, society and nature. But patriarchal society split them into opposite male-female polarities. Neumann must distort the content of the Great Mother image accordingly.

Likewise the maiden is a symbol of the marriage partner of the hero. She is dependent for her being upon the hero, who rescues her from the Great Mother. But no such symbol of the relation of the virgin goddess to the Great Mother exists in actual mother religion. The rescue of the maiden from the tower is a medieval myth. In Near Eastern and Greek mythology, however, even though the virgin goddess has been taken over by a male culture as the helper in its adventures, nevertheless she still retains her evolutionary origins in the Great Mother. It is not the hero who rescues the maiden, but rather, the virgin goddess (as representative of the mother goddess) who rescues the hero, overwhelmed annually by the powers of death. It is she who descends to the underworld to resurrect him from the death. It is she who then takes the initiative in the *hieros gamos* that saves the world (nature and society) from chaos and destruction. But Neumann's concept of the auxiliary character of the feminine cannot encompass this role of the maiden goddess and so must repress it for the more strictly patriarchal myth of the rescue of the maiden by the hero.

But, finally and most importantly, we must recognize the essentially patriarchal character of this entire description, in its normative definition of the ego or hero as male. In effect, all the feminine symbols here appear as auxiliaries of a male-centered ego development, which happens exclusively in males. The highest symbols to which woman can aspire, the anima sister or even Sophia, essentially exist as the context and helpers of a male hero adventure. At no point does the daughter of the Great Mother appear as adventurer in her own right. No helper, male or female, appears to aid her in her dragon fight or her effort to establish the meaning of her own autonomous existence. Neumann has given us, not the origin and history of consciousness per se, but the origin and history of consciousness under the conditions of male domination. Although this may be the only history of consciousness known to us so far, it cannot be accepted as the only history that is possible. In prepatriarchal myth, one discerns the rudimentary elements of what might have been an alternative history, based on dialectical interplay of the polarities of existence, rather than hierarchical dualism, which defines the "feminine" as the unconscious side of the self. Nor can it be accepted as the only kind of consciousness possible today when women, in asserting their right to autonomous existence, must re-examine the very definitions of ego and selfhood as these have developed in an androcentric culture.

The Jungian description of the self leaves women in a dilemma. Why are ego and intelligence described as masculine; unconsciousness as feminine? This construct leaves women with two equally debilitating solutions (patriarchy, based on false dualisms, always leaves women with opposite, equally debilitating solutions). Either women can imagine that men and women have exactly the same structure of consciousness, their ego also being "masculine," their unconsciousness "feminine"— in other words, women become persons by becoming male identified and regarding the "feminine" characteristics as secondary and auxiliary—or else the sex-stereotyping of psychic qualities ends by suggesting that women actually should aspire to a different personality and social roles from men, the motherly and sisterly auxiliary roles. Not for them is the hero adventure. Jung seemed to believe that woman's developed selfhood necessarily has a different tonality from that of the male, since for her the anima or intuitive self is the dominant self. The animus, for women, is a shadow self, and so intellectual women were limited to a strident and opinionated intellectuality. For men, however, the animus or intellectual self is the dominant self into which they integrate the poetic, intuitive side.[18] Neumann disagreed with this idea of a reversed relation of animus-anima in women and men. He believed that, in patriarchal society, women have exactly the same psychic structure as men, with a masculine ego and feminine unconscious.[19] These alternatives reveal to what extent the terms of Jungian psychology are defined in an androcentric culture, where intelligence and consciousness are identified with masculinity.

There does not yet exist any truly feminist psychoanalysis or therapy. The existing schools, basically, have analyzed psychic development within patriarchy and created therapies that reinforce male domination. Critical psychologists have got only far enough to reveal the male, ideological character of these descriptions of psychic phenomena as a reflection of male power-relations over women. But we have barely begun to uncover what is concealed under these male projections. What are the processes of the formation of the male ego that necessitate these repressive views of women? This too is still a male issue.

How women continue to experience themselves autonomously and struggle against this male subjugation of their experience is hardly known. What women might be like, how we would symbolize the polarities of self and other, thinking and feeling, activity and receptivity outside these traditions of male domination is something that we cannot know until a nonsexist society is created where women are recognized as full human persons, with a right to develop their potency not only for others, but for their own self-fulfillment. Women cannot accept either of the false alternatives of androcentric society. They can neither resign themselves to the "feminine" role or define their egos through a "masculine" identity. They must reconstitute all the terms of the process, so that all relations within the self and between the self and the others assumes a new content and a new mode of interaction. Feminism is truly a venture into a *terra incognita*. It must not only seek the reshaping of social relations for a humanized world. It must simultaneously create the therapy for a new selfhood of women and men appropriate to a humanized world.

Notes

1. Erik Erikson, "Inner Space," in *Identity, Youth and Crisis* (New York: Norton, 1963), chap. 7.
2. Sigmund Freud, "Three Essays on the Theory of Sexuality" (1905), *Standard Edition of the Complete Psychological Works of Sigmund Freud* (London: Hogarth Press, 1953), vol. 7. "Some Psychological Consequences of the Anatomical Distinctions between the Sexes" (1925), *Standard Edition* (1961), vol. 19. "Female Sexuality" (1931), *Standard Edition* (1961), vol. 21. "Femininity" (1931), from *New Introductory Lectures in Psychoanalysis, Standard Edition*, vol. 22.
3. Freud, *New Introductory Lectures*, pp. 125–26.
4. *Ibid.*, pp. 172–73.
5. *Ibid.*, pp. 125–26.
6. Helene Deutsch, *The Psychology of Women: A Psychoanalytic Interpretation* (New York: Grune and Statton, 1944–45), vols. 1 and 2. I am indebted for this analysis to James W. Anderson, a student at Harvard Divinity School, whose unpublished paper on Helene Deutsch's *Psychology of Women* was written for my class on Sexism and Contemporary Ideologies, December 1973.
7. A. Adler, "Sex," in *Understanding Human Nature* (1927).
8. Karen Horney, "Flight from Womanhood" (1917), in *Psychoanalysis and Women*, ed. J. B. Miller (New York: Penguin, 1973), pp. 5–20.
9. Karen Horney, *Feminine Psychology* (New York: Norton,1967), pp. 107–18 (originally written in 1930).
10. William Masters and Virginia E. Johnson, *Human Sexual Response* (Boston: Little, Brown, 1966).
11. Mary Jane Sherfey, *The Nature and Evolution of Female Sexuality* (New York: Random House, 1972).
12. Theodore Reik, *The Making of Woman* (New York: McGraw-Hill, 1973).
13. Phyllis Chesler, *Women and Madness* (New York: Avon, 1972).

14. Juliet Mitchell, *Psychoanalysis and Feminism* (New York: Pantheon, 1974).
15. F. Nietzsche, "Woman," in *Beyond Good and Evil*, trans. W. Kaufmann (New York: Random House, 1966), pp. 231–39; A. Schopenhauer, "On Woman," in *Studies in Pessimism*, chap. 7; see Philip Rieff, *Freud: The Mind of the Moralist* (Garden City, N.Y.: Doubleday, 1961), pp. 200–2.
16. C. G. Jung, "On the Anima" and "On the Mother Archetype," in *Archetypes and the Collective Unconsciousness* (*Collected Works*, vol. 9) (Princeton, N.J.: Princeton University Press, 1969); and *Symbols of Transformation* (*Collected Works*, vol. 5) Princeton, N.J.: Princeton University Press, 1967).
17. Princeton University Press, 1954, 1955: Bollingen Series, vols. 42 and 47.
18. C. G. Jung, *Psyche and Symbol* (New York: Doubleday, 1958), pp. 9–22.
19. E. Neumann, *The Origins and History of Consciousness* (Princeton: Princeton University Press, 1954), pp. 402–18, and 125, n. 13.

The First and Final Proletariat: Socialism and Feminism

IF PSYCHOANALYSIS HAS BEEN THE AMBIGUOUS TOOL OF PER-sonal liberation in modern society, communism remains the primary ideology of socioeconomic liberation. It is to this tradition that I now turn to discuss the social dimension of feminism. Feminism itself arose in the late eighteenth century as a part of the ideology of liberalism. The utopian socialists took over this concern with women as a part of their rethinking of the family, the local community, and the state. The Owenites and the St. Simonians established in the 1840s what were regarded as sensationally radical theories of women's liberation. In this period feminism was identified with socialism. Middle-class feminists in England and America felt called upon continually to defend traditional concepts of the family and the female role in order to counteract this presumed relation of feminism to the socialist critique of the family.[1]

UTOPIAN SOCIALISM AND WOMEN

The views of the utopian socialists on women and the family were, however, a confused array of radical, romantic, and reactionary ideas. Anarchists such as Proudhon followed Rousseau in combining primitivism with rigid patriarchalism, decreeing that women existed solely to serve every need and whim of the male.[2] Proudhon's desire to abolish the state only put all authority back into the hands of the patriarchal lord of the family. Since French unionism took its line from Proudhon, this has effectively pushed aside the drive for equality for women in the program of worker's rights. The union movement generally reacted negatively to the fact that women were used by industry as a cheap labor force, hired for a fraction of male wages, worked long hours at backbreaking, monotonous tasks, and were fired at will. Instead of regarding women as a group to be organized against this exploitation, they were viewed by male unionists as a competitive threat to male wages, to be eliminated or separated into different work.

Other early socialists, such as Fourier, paralleled the ideas of the French libertine tradition, exemplified at its extreme by the Marquis de Sade, in confusing women's liberation with sexual libertinism.[3] This tradition is also followed by post-Freudian socialists, such as Wilhelm Reich and Herbert Marcuse. Like Fourier, they imagine the Age of Liberty to be a flowering of love freed from sexually repressive authoritarianism and alienated labor.[4] Fourier proposed a communalized form of social life that would free women from economic dependency and allow everyone, even children, to choose the employments that naturally attracted them. Fourier proposed that the measure of a society's progress could be discerned by the extent to which it freed women from brutalization.[5] However, this could be understood in a radical or a conservative way. Auguste Comte, the theoretician of positivism, interpreted this to mean that the degree of progress in a society can be measured by the extent to which it eliminates women from production and confines them to the home where they are to be enshrined as the symbol and nurturer of the sympathetic principle in human relations. Comte's concept of the role of women in Positivism is built on the romantic doctrine of complementarity and is an early statement of the bourgeois cult of the leisured lady as the symbol of the affluence of the male industrialist.[6]

The St. Simonians gathered up these doctrines in a confused way. They demanded the liberation of women from patriarchal power and the sequestered life in the home, the right of divorce and free love. Women should be integrated into all the elites of the new scientific, industrial society. They proclaimed the reclamation of the flesh from sexual repression. The liberation of women represents the restitution of the emotional, sensual, and material principles from their long repression by Christianity. Like many males today who regard themselves as sympathizers with women's liberation, they were primarily concerned with the liberation of the repressed, "feminine side" of men in a way that reinforced the stereotypic differences between male and female "natures." The St. Simonians believed that every elite should be represented by both a male and a female leader to symbolize this restoration of the "feminine side" of life. The highest role of the Supreme Father, the papacy of St. Simonianism, must be complemented by the Supreme Mother, who would take her seat at his right hand. Their feminism thus was a secularized Mariology, just as their general concepts of a new priesthood and cult of secular society were modeled after Catholicism.

The St. Simonians announced the imminent advent of a female messiah who would appear somewhere in the East and would dictate what steps were necessary for the liberation and integration of the feminine principle into society. Their doctrines of female liberation were confused with free love and scandalized all France. The leaders of the movement were put on trial for undermining social morality. In a spectacular show trial, they insisted on putting forth their views on liberated women and would have only women appear as their lawyers. Women were, of course, forbidden at this time to appear in court as lawyers. The leaders were convicted, and the movement peaked in this spectacular event. (Its followers dissipated their energies afterward in trips to the Levant in search of the female messiah reputed to be hidden in a harem there.) In spite of these idiosyncrasies, the St. Simonian movement attracted the most radical feminists of the day, who produced a deluge of articles and manifestos on the condition of women, published in newspapers such as *La Femme Libre* between 1830 and 1833.[7]

This mixture of mystical, mariological, and radical social themes was typical of the times. The Shakers, in a similar period, declared that God had been incarnated in the female messiah, Mother Anne, whose appearance was necessary to complement and complete the revelation of God in the male messiah, Jesus. Salvation could not be completed as long as there was only a male messiah. Only with the female messiah could women and the "feminine half of men" be redeemed and the promised salvation fulfilled. In the Shaker Scriptures all the feminine sophiological, ecclesiological, and mariological passages are developed into a masterful hermeneutic to demonstrate the need and even the prediction of this complementary incarnation of God in female form. The Shakers said that every level of spiritual reality, starting with God, is androgynous. Salvation can be complete only when this androgynous nature of spiritual reality is fully realized in creation.[8]

The New England transcendentalists also toyed with ideas of a female messiah, an idea that cropped up in a number of different movements in the 1830s in both Europe and America. Both the Shaker and the transcendentalist views on this found their way into Christian Science, as well as into the many female-founded religious movements and missions of female prophets of the nineteenth century.[9] The 1830s to 1840s was also the heyday of utopian experimentation in America. Most of the movements thought that the abolition of private property must be completed by the abolition of the private-property relation of women to men in the nuclear family. Some thought this should be done through celibacy and a "spiritual marriage" of the whole community to each other (these celibate communities being generally heterosexual). But a few thought this should take the form of literal group marriage. The Oneida Community in upstate New York was the most daring experimentation with group marriage.[10]

THE MARXIST ANALYSIS OF THE SUBJUGATION OF WOMEN

Neither Marx nor Engels were, at first, disposed to include this criticism of the family in what they saw as "scientific socialism," to distinguish it from the romanticism of the utopian socialists. However, Marx was impressed by Fourier's principle that progress in society is measured by the extent to which it liberates women. But he, like Comte, was originally disposed to interpret this as meaning the extent to which it rescues the woman, as the weaker and more delicate partner, from brutalizing labor and establishes over her a benevolent protection. However, their study of the British working class convinced Marx and Engels that this view of women was actually a class myth. The working-class woman demonstrated that women were capable of the hardest labor, while also assuming the double burden of the household. The myth of the delicate lady is a bourgeois fiction that rationalizes a property-and-dependency relation, while ignoring the way this class ideal is itself erected on the backs of working-class men and women.

Engels and Marx also concluded that industrial labor, despite its initially brutal conditions (doubly so for women), was also providing the conditions which would emancipate women. Industrialism would restore to women an economic autonomy vis-à-vis the male by giving them independent jobs and incomes outside the home.[11] Marx and Engels came across the work of anthropologists, such as Bachofen and Morgan, who proposed the thesis that a matriarchal, communist state of society had preceded patriarchal society and private property. This shook their assumptions that the patriarchal family was the primordial form of social relations. All these influences flowed together into Engels's foundational treatise on the subjugation and the emancipation of women in *The Origin and History of the Family, Private Property and the State*, which he planned together with Marx, but completed and published in 1884 after Marx's death.[12]

This work by Engels, despite its oversimplifications, continues to be the basis for socialist doctrines of women's liberation. Feminists today who seek to go beyond reformist strategies and to envision a reconstructed society and family as the basis of women's liberation, must still go back to it as a primary text.

Engels accepted from Bachofen and other theoreticians of the thesis of "primitive matriarchy" an evolutionary concept of society. The earliest state of humanity was believed to be that of the primal horde practicing generalized promiscuity. This stage was overcome by the matriarchal stage of primitive communism. Matriarchy was not understood as female domination comparable to patriarchy, but rather, was understood as a matrilineal form of organization where property was held in common and which corresponded to an equalitarian relation between men and women prior to the development of class stratification. The women remained in her own tribe and all her children were counted as members of her clan. This allowed the "pairing marriage" where men and women could mate according to personal inclination and dissolve their relation freely without the double standard and dependency that became imposed on women under patriarchy. Without private property to inherit, there is no concern to differentiate legitimate from illegitimate children. The principle of paternity remains vague, and all children are equally members of the maternal clan.

The overthrow of mother right corresponded to the increase in wealth and the institution of private property. Now the male wished only his own children, especially the male heirs, to be recognized. The woman then must be subjugated to the monogamous marriage as herself a piece of private property, strictly excluded from all other sexual relations, so that he can be sure that her children are his own. Patriarchal marriage creates the distinction of legitimate and illegitimate children and hedges in the married woman with strict sanctions against infidelity, to ensure the principle of paternity. But patriarchal monogamy assumes the double standard because the male remains sexually free. The concubine and the prostitute become the second-class females who serve a male sexuality that remains promiscuous, but whose bastard children pass into the servant class. In Engels's dramatic language:

> The overthrow of Mother Right was the world historic defeat of the female sex. The man seized the reins of the house also. The woman was degraded, enthralled, the slave of man's lust, a mere instrument for breeding children. . . .
>
> Thus monogamy does not by any means make its appearance in history as the reconciliation of man and woman, still less as the highest form of such reconciliation. On the contrary, it appears as the subjugation of one sex by the other, as the proclamation of a conflict between the sexes, entirely unknown hitherto in prehistoric times. . . . The first class antagonism which appears in history coincides with the antagonism between man and woman in monogamous marriage and the first class oppression is represented by the female sex. . . . It inaugurated, along with slavery and private wealth, that epoch, lasting until today, in which every advance is likewise a relative regression, in which the well being and development of one group are attained by the misery and repression of the other. It is the cellular form of class society, in which we can study the nature of the antagonisms and contradictions which develop fully in the latter.[13]

Engels believed that a higher ideal was established in Protestantism in the form of the love marriage. This, in principle, demanded fidelity by both husband and wife, and free choice, which presumes an emotional equality of the woman in the partnership. But Protestantism continued to be based on the bourgeois property relation, so in practice this principle only exacerbated the hypocrisy. The theoretical principle of emotional equality was subverted in practice, since the woman must sell her sexuality for economic security in the property relation of marriage. The husband, who must achieve economic success before marriage in order to develop the property for marriage and children, postpones marriage and takes relief in prostitutes.

Only in the working class is this hypocrisy dissolved, Engels felt, because they have no property to pass on. Since both men and women are employed, the woman has the economic autonomy to enter into a free-love contract. Thus Engels postulated that the bourgeois family was dissolving in the industrial proletariat. The ancient free marriage or pairing marriage, entered into for no reasons other than mutual emotional satisfaction and freely dissolved by mutual consent, which existed in primitive matriarchal times, was now reappearing in the proletariat. Industrialism begins the liberation of women, despite its exploitative conditions, which weigh doubly heavily on women. Women recover the economic autonomy lost to them in primitive times, when they were subjugated to the patriarchal property relationship. This economic autonomy, as it grows and overcomes injustice in wages and working conditions, will be the basis of all other freedoms for women, including their right to dispose of their sexuality by free choice rather than coercion.

Engels's thesis that the bourgeois marriage was dissolving in the proletariat was a false prediction which was of a piece with the Marxist confusion of the primitive, chaotic conditions of the birth of capitalism with its death knell. He believed that capitalism would progressively depress the majority of the population while enriching a smaller and smaller elite until the great majority would revolt and seize the means of production, collectivizing them for the well-being of all. Marxism underestimated the ability of capitalism to assimilate the working class and unionism into neo-mercantilist or state capitalism as an organ of capitalism itself. Likewise he underestimated the capacity of improving conditions of life to inculcate middle-class-family values into the working class, making them the last and most ardent defenders of patriarchal and puritanical mores. The kind of destruction of the middle-class family, which he described in the early working class, today would appear only in the unemployed and marginal sections of society.

Engels believed that communism would establish the complete equality of men and women in both society and sexuality. Women would receive the same education and choose whatever work in society they wished. Women would be liberated to work in all spheres of productive activity equally with men. This role in production, giving women economic independence, would be the foundation of their liberation in communist society. Economic independence would then found their sexual independence. They would no longer have to sell their sexuality for economic security, have their income and inheritance the property of their husbands, be coerced into marriage along class lines by their parents, or kept in marriages, grown cold, by economic need. Marriage under communism could then be allowed to return to the "pairing marriage" as a personal love contract between two persons on the basis of compatibility, entered into and dissolved without economic considerations.

Engels denied that this would lead to libertine behavior. On the contrary, he believed that the natural instincts of mankind were monogamous. If couples were allowed to enter a relationship on the basis of love and compatibility, rather than coerced by economic need, the hypocrisy of infidelity and the need for multiple relationships would disappear. Truly compatible relations would be lifelong stable relations. Engels sees marriage under communism as the flowering of the (bourgeois) ideal of faithful, lifelong love contracts. He did not consider to what extent the very concept of exclusivity in monogamy might itself be a reflection of a property relationship of sexuality. Confidently he declared, "Since sex love is by its nature exclusive—although this exclusiveness is fully realized today only in the woman—then marriage based on sex love is by its nature monogamy" [14]

The Marxist movement was harshly critical of bourgeois feminism, just as it was of bourgeois unionism. Rival theories of sexual liberation and the liberation of women, which did not challenge the economic contradictions between the middle class and the workers, were regarded as incipiently reactionary.[15] The suffragette movement was condemned as a middle-class phenomenon, which was working only to secure for the women of the dominant class the legal and social rights enjoyed as class privileges by the males of their group. It failed to see the way these rights were themselves based on the exploitation of the working class. The woman who wanted to vote, to go to the university, and to enter the professions basically wanted an equal share in the propertied privileges of her class. She would vote in a system which itself expressed the class power of the bourgeois. Marxist feminists such as Emma Goldmann and union organizers such as Mother Jones stood aside from that women's movement which concerned itself primarily with the vote.

This Marxist criticism of bourgeois feminism proved by no means inaccurate. The earlier feminists had demanded the vote on the basis of a principle of equality between all persons in the society. But, as I have shown earlier, by the last quarter of the nineteenth century in the United States this principle had become corrupted into a demand for the vote for white middle-class Protestant women, rationalizing at the same time the denial of the vote to blacks and working-class immigrants who were usually Catholics or Jews. They allowed the suffragette movement to become a reconsolidation of the rule of the WASP elite over the inferior "masses." In short, bourgeois feminism tended to sell out to a class and racist line of argument in order to win approbation from male legislators.[16]

Marxism also was critical of the confusion of the liberation of women with sexual liberation. Marxism gravitated toward a morality of puritanical self-discipline, including sexual discipline, as the natural and proper morality of the virtuous proletariat. Talk of liberating people from sexual repression, all forms of bohemian sexual experimentation, was bourgeois degeneracy. Lenin was equally suspicious of the concern of feminists with consciousness-raising and the personal, psychological side of sexism. The Freudian movement also was lumped with the culture of "bourgeois degeneracy." Paradoxically, Marxism exalted the puritanism of the early bourgeois as the essential hallmark of proletarian morality.[17]

However, Lenin was not entirely misguided in suspecting in Freud reactionary tendencies, although this lay more with his patriarchal authoritarianism than with his concern with sexual repression. More to the point, Lenin recognized in the bohemian element in the revolutionary youth an exploitative libertinism that had little to do with the liberation of women. He saw that sexual liberation without the liberation of women from social inferiority and economic dependency was merely the underside of the present status of women as sexual objects. Without economic equality, women could not enter into such relationships as equal partners. The liberation of women must be founded on their economic autonomy and equality as producers. Only then could there be a sexual liberation that was dignified and nonexploitative. Only after the communist revolution could sex love become genuinely the free choice of adult persons. This freedom would be founded on the revolution in ownership and organization of production that would give the female equal economic independence with the male.

These suspicions of a sexual liberation without economic liberation were borne out by the revolt of feminists from the New Left in the 1960s. American feminists discovered all over again that sexual liberation does not end sexism, if male leftists continue to assume their own right to dominate the roles of power, relegating women to auxiliary service roles as coffee makers, envelope lickers, and bedwarmers. Yet Lenin's rejection of the psychoanalytical revolution, and his confusion of feminist consciousness-raising with bourgeois feminism and sexual libertinism, left Marxism with a superficial view of the nature of sexism which became apparent in the subsequent communist revolutions.

WOMEN'S LIBERATION AND COMMUNIST REVOLUTIONS

Marx and Engels believed that the communist revolution would take place in Western Europe as the final stage of transformation of society beyond the highest development of capitalism. When they projected the liberation of women through industrialism, finally culminating in the communist revolution that would create the society of realized equality, they presumed that communist society would be building upon all the advances made by women in work, education, and social development of the family in Western Europe. However, the communist revolutions have not taken place in industrial countries, but in the preindustrialized feudal countries of Russia, China, South Asia, and Cuba, where woman's position was still like that of the Middle Ages. Here women had no legal rights, could be beaten, sold, or even killed by their male relatives. There was little tradition of women either in universities or in skilled industrial work. Making the socialist revolution in these countries had to begin with making the industrial revolution under collectivized conditions. The mystification of what is involved in a socialist revolution derives from the fact that communist revolutions have been applying to the tasks of industrialization and national liberation from Western colonialism a Marxist language which was originally envisioned for a quite different stage of socioeconomic development.

The accomplishments and the limitations of the liberation of women in communist revolution, however, must be measured by the fact that these revolutions had to start with a much different status of women than that envisioned in Engels's treatise. The leisured affluence and segregation from productive work which was characteristic of Western bourgeois women would have been available only to a small circle of aristocrats and courtesans in these feudal societies. On the other hand, Russian peasant women, especially in the eastern regions of the USSR and in China still existed under conditions of direct enslavement, ignorance, and lack of elementary human rights unknown to Western women. In Russian peasant families it was customary for the bride's father to give the bridegroom a new whip, which was hung over the bed to symbolize the transfer of authority from the father to the husband, an authority comparable to the ownership of a slave. Women possessed no legal rights to work, travel, or engage in any activity without the permission of husband or father.

In China before the revolution the position of ordinary women was, if anything, even more comparable to that of a slave. Women worked ceaselessly, and could be beaten and even killed without redress. Polygamy, concubinage, and the selling of women into marriage or prostitution were common. She could inherit no property. Footbinding symbolized the reduction of the upper-class woman to ornamental status. Marriages were arranged by the families with little regard for the desires of the woman. The upper-class woman must compete with rival wives and concubines for her husband's affections. To societies such as these the Marxist doctrines on the liberation of women came as an explosive eruption in social patterns that were thousands of years old.[18] Measured by the distance between bourgeois feminism in the West and Marxist feminism in Russia and China, the communist achievement is still an impressive attempt to create the conditions which would liberate women from some of their housekeeping and child-care chores in order that they could compete more equally with men on the work force. Such aids as nationalized child-care centers, maternity leave with guaranteed re-employment, and communal kitchens are the social preconditions for the equality of women in the economy which Western capitalist society is still not willing to accept. But, when judged by the distance between the present status of women in these communist societies and their prerevolutionary condition, the transformation in the role of women created by the communist societies is nothing less than the leap of a millennium of social change.

No demand appeared so radical or caused so much social tension as the changes which the communists made in the status of women in the first ten years of the Russian revolution and, similarly, in China. Within six weeks after the Russian revolution the ecclesiastical control of marriage was replaced by civil registration. A new matrimonial code was promulgated that established complete legal and economic equality between husband and wife, the dissolution of the distinction between legitimate and illegitimate children and between legal and common-law marriages. Women could decide on their own names, citizenship, and place of residence. Marriage was entered into or dissolved by mutual consent. Property was divided equally. The struggle against prostitution, the development of child-care and communal kitchens and laundries, the legalization of abortion—all were intended to create the conditions for women's real growth toward equality. Nor was this development merely left to party decisions. Women's units were created which were intended to organize all women into groups for self-education and political struggle to attain these rights. So threatening did these political education meetings for women appear that not a few women were kidnapped, beaten, or killed by their male relatives when they attempted to attend these meetings.[19]

In China the changes created in the status of women after the revolution were no less explosive, amounting to a systematic abolition of the traditional Chinese family. These took the form of land reform, revolutionary marriage law, and the communalization of work and the home. Article Six of the Constitution, adopted in September 1946, declared: "The People's Republic of China abolishes the feudal system which holds women in bondage. Women shall enjoy equal rights with men in political, economic, cultural, educational, and social life. Freedom of marriage for men and women shall be enforced." All forms of bigamy, concubinage, and forced marriage were abolished. Divorce was to be granted by mutual consent. However, systematic communalization of work conditions and the home, which have been carried out much more radically in China than in Russia, have been the social basis for equality of men and women on the job and in their personal relations.[20]

Western observers have recently begun to take notice of these developments. While praising the Chinese efforts to create the social conditions for women's liberation in the home/work relations, they often find strange the fierce asceticism and desexualizing of male and female relations in China, which contrasts so strongly with the pervasive eroticism of Western culture. The new Chinese appear to believe that the ideal marriage should be based on mutual ideological rectitude and high work quotas by both spouses and in no way on mutual sexual attractiveness. However, this fierce asceticism must be placed in the context of a society where, traditionally, woman's subjugation depended on the treatment of women as sex objects, and where the double standard reduced large numbers of women to living by prostitution. The Chinese seem to be saying that the retraining of men and women to regard each other primarily as human beings, as comrades of the mind and colleagues on the job, depends on a fierce repression of the tradition which related women to men primarily as sexual objects.

In Russia the first ten years of rapid social transformation in the status of women was partially replaced in the thirties by a reversion to more traditional concepts of the family and woman's role as wife and mother, along with similar reversions to authoritarianism in all other spheres under Stalinism. The Russian experiment was brought short with a certain formal equality on the job, while retaining essentially the traditional bourgeois concept of the family, somewhat alleviated by institutions such as child care. In practical terms, this meant that, although women work much more generally throughout the professions in Russia, they are handicapped on the job by the tasks of housework and food procurement, which are in no way shared by the male. The basic sexist psychology of the woman as servant of the man in the home was left intact, its psychological mechanisms left unexplored. Since advancement on the job was measured in terms of work quotas, while the woman's work in the home remained uncounted as a part of her work load, this means that the married woman with children carried a double load.

In 1934 homosexuality was made a crime again. Two years later abortion was made illegal, and new laws reversed many of the provisions of the marriage code of 1920. These laws re-established the distinction between illegitimate and legitimate children and made divorce more difficult. The advances made before were not entirely undone, but they were now to be contained within a firmly paternalistic concept of the family and the structure of leadership in the society. The devastations wrought by the Second World War further increased the pressure on women to bear children for the nation. At the same time, the increasing depersonalization of public society made the family the one unit in society into which people could retreat for personal care and affection. With de-Stalinization in 1955, abortion again became legal and birth-control advice freely available. The right to divorce was eased. But there seems little possibility of a general reopening of the question of the liberation of women apart from the larger struggle to liberalize Soviet society as a whole.[21]

By contrast, the drive for full equality for women in China shows no signs of stopping with a formal equality before the law which does not take into consideration the concrete handicaps of women, as women, in the home. The Chinese inherit the Leninist system of centralism and ideological unity. But they have concentrated the struggle for socialism on communalization and direct participation at the level of the local communities. This is the sphere where women are traditionally left at a disadvantage. Moreover, the Chinese have engaged in a prolonged cultural revolution intended to tear down and overthrow the psychological structures of hierarchicalism and elitism. The traditional elites of society have been forced to rub their noses in the dirt of peasant labor, while the traditionally subordinate groups have been encouraged to criticize tendencies to elitism in the former mandarins. Students criticize teachers; peasants, city folk; nurses, doctors; children, parents. This is intended to create a revolution in consciousness which destroys the traditional orders of authority and creates direct participation at the base. Women, the oldest subordinate in every hierarchy, find ample encouragement to struggle against every manifestation of chauvinism. The communalization of the functions of the home and their integration with the job create the concrete social conditions which allow women to function as equals on the job. Emancipation is seen as a continual struggle to create a new culture, a new psychology, as well as a new social order. Continual self-criticism in the local cadres allow women to bring up newly perceived evidences of disadvantages as they encounter them.

Chinese Marxism is criticized in the West for its authoritarianism and sexual repressiveness. However, since it is women's liberation which is in accord with the correct Maoist line, this authoritarianism gives women an immense advantage. It would be the male who would have to acknowledge his incorrectness if he were to be convicted of chauvinist ways of thinking. The asceticism of the Chinese Marxists illustrates the extent to which communism enshrines the sexually repressed personality of early Calvinism as its way of maximizing social energies. While this may be a loss to the projects of individualist poetry, aestheticism, and the integration of self and body, in the concrete context of liberating women from their traditional subjugation as sex objects it is immensely useful. By dogmatically repressing the experience of men and women as sexual opposites, men are forced to deal with women solely as persons who are identical with themselves as thinkers and workers. Sexual neutralization in this sense operates in the service of equalization. Before Western critics would demand that values of individualism, dissent, and aestheticism be recognized, it must ask itself much more seriously how these values are integrated into a culture of equality.

Feminism in the West must take seriously a socialist dimension of the women's movement. Without creating the socioeconomic conditions for equality, the rights earned by feminists remain middle-class privileges for those women who are either childless or who can afford to pay a housekeeper and nursemaid. The vast majority of women will remain tied to their traditional caste roles as the auxiliary support system of male work, both at home and on the job, no matter how many equal rights are earned for them on the books or how many professions some women manage to invade as token representatives. Liberal feminism remains token feminism. It cannot effect the caste status of the mass of women.

Marxist feminism today is especially concentrating on the critique of the economic function of housework. This is where women appear as the final proletariat or even as the last slave, whose unpaid labor goes unrecognized and uncounted in the analyses of work, and yet which forms the material base for time and energy released for all other forms of work. Housework, or the "second shift" traditionally done by women, is the invisible economic base of male autonomy, mobility, and concentrated energy at work. This second shift keeps women tied to the home and to menial marginal work jobs that can be combined with the tasks of the home. No person who does heavy labor or engages in intense executive roles demanding long hours, continuous concentration, and mobility can also be expected to be able to return continually to the home to do several more hours a day of domestic drudgery or to spend time in long lines to buy food or merchandise. Women cannot be equal on the job according to their true abilities until they are truly freed from the second shift through collectivization and professionalization of these tasks by society and/or the distribution of these tasks equally between men and women and between persons in every form of employment, i.e., the abolition of both sex and class structures. As long as all jobs, and especially the more demanding and prestigious jobs, are based on having a wife, plus a battalion of invisible female support staff on the job, women cannot be equal on the job, despite all fictions of equal opportunities. This abolition of the second shift for women cannot be left to the private arrangements of individual couples. It must be socially institutionalized in a transformed home/work relation.

But feminism must also explore the cultural psychology of housework. It is in this arena that women are not only exhausted physically and rendered unfit for the more demanding and more mobile work of the leadership group. Here also the basic model of woman as the "shitworker" of society is created and daily reinforced. Even the jobs she is given in the work force will tend to belong primarily to the same category of shitwork. Women at work form the auxiliary support system for male executive roles. Here the psychology of sexism finds its last frontier, rationalizing women's role in reproduction into a lifetime of child-raising and domestic chores. It is here that women are made to be distracted and diffuse, while men are freed for monolithic concentration, without concern for the bodily structures which support this concentration.

Since women's work is invisible and, at the base, unpaid, this handicap upon women will be rationalized as a difference of nature and temperament, dictated by biology rather than recognized as the effects of a systemic work relation. The educational and cultural apparatus of society will continue to be bent to forcing women to be resigned to this role, as their nature and destiny, and to tailor their expectations accordingly. Males will be taught to be the adventurers and world conquerers, without noticing the way these roles are erected upon a pyramid of female labor. There can be no liberation of women as a caste, no flowering of female energies commensurate with her potential, until this invisible economic relation of women to men, and the cultural psychology it demands, are overcome.[22]

However, while feminists must recognize the need for a socialist dimension, feminism must ask itself whether the Marxist exaltation of sexual repression, the work ethic, and class conflict can represent ultimate values. Much is sacrificed in individuality, feeling, and spiritual interiority for social equality. Is there another way, especially for Western society, to work toward social justice for women, as well as repressed classes and races, while integrating these deeply held values? Is there a way of communalizing society in freer local communities which preserves individual differences and does not need the rigid Leninist pattern of party centralization culminating in the rule of a god-king? Is the endless prolongation of models of life drawn from warfare and industrial labor the best we can do in envisioning a liberated society?

Sexism must be seen as the expression of a primal psychology of domination and repression forged in the one-sided emergence of the male in the struggle for survival. The life of sensuousness, celebration, leisure, free creativity, and exploration of feelings was allowed a small elite class, who stood on the backs of the toiling masses. Sexism was the first and basic model for this subjugation of one part of the race to bodily work, so that the other part could be free to create and enjoy. Socialism must go beyond a mere generalization of repression, misery, and work if it is to be a vision of liberation. It must recover those dreams of liberated creativity which Marx shared with the utopians and anarchists: the vision of a society in which the basic necessities of life have been conquered to such an extent as to free all persons for a life with room for celebration, free creativity, the reintegration of mind and body, the de-alienation of work, the overcoming of the split between work and pleasure.[23]

Is such a society possible? Our present Western type of society, which I shall discuss at greater length in the next chapter, is based on exploitation of people by people and the rape of the earth, and is rapidly eating up the resources for a postscarcity communism. The hopes of all oppressed peoples for wider opportunities through expanding production stand to be cheated by such a system. All the crises of history are converging: racism, sexism, colonialism, the technological depletion of the earth. The scientific knowledge for an ecological technology, based on renewable energy resources, the reintegration of farm and town, home and work in a pattern of diversity and balance modeled after ecological systems—this theoretically is not beyond our grasp. But the social structures and psychology of historical oppressive power; the legacy of class, racist, imperialist, and sexist structures of domination raise obstacles against a humanistic implementation of such possibilities, which we do not yet know how to begin to overcome.

Notes

1. Aileen Kraditor, *The Ideas of the Woman Suffrage Movement, 1890–1920* (Garden City, N.Y.: Doubleday, 1971), p. 21.
2. P. J. Proudhon, "Love and Marriage," *Selected Writings* (Garden City, N.Y.: Doubleday, 1969).
3. See D. Diderot, "Love in Tahiti" and the Marquis de Sade, "A Bedroom Discourse," in *French Utopias*, ed. F. E. and F. P. Manuel (New York: Free Press, 1966), pp. 149ff., 217ff.
4. H. Marcuse, *Eros and Civilization* (New York: Random House, 1962). Wilhelm Reich, *Sex-Pol: Essays 1929–1934*, ed. Lee Baxandall (New York: Vintage Books, 1972).
5. Charles Fourier, "Of the Condition of Women," in *Design for Utopia, Selected Writings* (New York: Schocken, 1971).
6. Auguste Comte, "The Influence of Positivism on Women," in *A General View of Positivism* (Paris, 1848), pp. 227–303; also T. Veblen, *The Theory of the Leisure Class* (1899).
7. The St. Simonian School, "The Emancipation of Women," in *French Utopias*, pp. 293ff; also "The Emancipation of Women" in Richard Pankhurst, *The Saint Simonians, Mill and Carlyle* (Atlantic Highlands, N.J.: Humanities, 1957), chap. 8.
8. *The Testimony of Christ's Second Appearing* (Shaker Bible), esp. Bk. 8, sec. 9 and Bk. 9, Pt. 11, secs. 1–3.
9. See Robert Peel, *Christian Science* (New York: Holt, Rinehart and Winston, 1958).
10. R. M. Kanter, *Commitment and Community, Communes and Utopias in Sociological Perspective* (Cambridge, Mass.: Harvard University Press, 1972), pp. 77–80.
11. Hal Draper, "Marx and Engels on the Women's Revolution," in Roberta Salper, *Female Liberation, History and Current Politics* (New York: Knopf, 1972), pp. 83–107.
12. J. J. Bachofen, *Myth, Religion and Mother Right* (1861); L. H. Morgan, *Ancient Society* (1877); R. Briffault, *The Matriarchal Theory of Social Origins* (1927).

13. F. Engels, *The Origins and History of the Family, Private Property and the State* (published in Zurich, 1884) (Boston: Free Press pamphlet of chaps. 1 and 2, pp. 65–66.
14. *Ibid.*, pp. 81–83. See August Bebel, *Women under Socialism* (published in German, 1883) (New York: Schocken, 1971).
15. Evelyn Reed, *Problems of Women's Liberation* (New York: Pathfinder Press, 1971), pp. 64ff., 77ff.
16. Kraditor, *op. cit.*, chaps. 6–7.
17. See Clara Zetkin, "Lenin on the Woman Question," in *The Emancipation of Women*, from the writings of V. I. Lenin (New York: International Publishers, 1934), pp. 95ff.
18. Sheila Rowbotham, *Women, Resistance and Revolution: A History of Women and Revolution in the Modern World* (New York: Random House, 1972), pp. 134–40; 170–83.
19. *Ibid.*, pp. 141–59.
20. *Ibid.*, pp. 184–99.
21. *Ibid., pp. 159–68; also Judith Merkle and Janet Salaff, "Women and Revolution: The Lessons of the Soviet Union and China," Socialist Revolution*, 1, no. 4 (October 1970).
22. Pat Mainardi, "The Politics of Housework," New England Free Press pamphlet; also Isabel Larguis and John Dumoulin, "Toward a Science of Women's Liberation," in *NACLA Newsletter*, 6, no. 10 (December 1972).
23. See Murray Bookchin, *Post-Scarcity Anarchism* (San Francisco: Ramparts Press, 1971), pp. 55–82.

New Woman and New Earth: Women, Ecology, and Social Revolution

SINCE WOMEN IN WESTERN CULTURE HAVE BEEN TRADITIONALLY identified with nature, and nature, in turn, has been seen as an object of domination by man (males), it would seem almost a truism that the mentality that regarded the natural environment as an object of domination drew upon imagery and attitudes based on male domination of women. William Leiss, in his study, *The Domination of Nature*, sees Francis Bacon as representing the transition from the earlier mythic and religious roots of the concept of domination of nature to its modern scientific, technological expression. Leiss notes the roots of the language of domination of nature in social domination. In Bacon particularly he notes that the "master of nature" is imaged as a patriarchal despot whose subjugation of nature is expressed in the language of domination over women and slaves:

> I am come in very truth, leading to you Nature with all her children to bind her to your service and make her your slave. *The Masculine Birth of Time*[1]

The language is both that of despotism and that of sexual aggression. Nature is pictured as a fecund female slave whose "children" are to be used by rulers by reducing her to a condition of total submission. Leiss regards the ecological crisis and the collapse of faith in scientific technology in the twentieth century as the results of this relationship of "use" of nature to social domination (although he relates this to class domination only). The productivity that resulted from the application of instrumentalist science to nature was fed into a magnification of the structures of social domination, rather than providing the basis for a postscarcity, equalitarian society. Is it enough then just to become socialists in our vision of the "exploitation" of the results of production for the good of "all people" in order to cure this disease? Or does the removal of the covert language of class domination from the project of domination of nature suggest the need for a new model of ecological relations as well? Finally, does the sexist relation between men and women, which Leiss ignores except for the one mention cited above, provide the hidden link between the two?

SEXISM AND DOMINATION OF NATURE IN PATRIARCHAL RELIGION

The social and symbolic roots of this view of the world as "rapine" are not easily sorted out. Since Lynn White's essay on "The Religious Roots of our Ecological Crisis," [2] it has been common to trace this view back to the Old Testament mandate that "man" subdue the earth and have dominion over the animals (Gen. 1:28). But this interpretation incorporates the Genesis language too directly into Christian and secular views of domination, based on splits between mind and body, society and nature, and is insensitive to the residue of earlier nature religion that still influences the view of nature found in the Old Testament. Unlike Christianity, Hebrew religion, especially in its pre-exilic period, is not a religion of alienation that views nature as inferior or evil. Like the Canaanite religion, which the Hebrews partly overthrew and partly assimilated, it is a religion of socionatural renewal. [3]

Society and nature cohere in a single created community under the sovereignty of God. The breaking of the covenant with God results both in a devastation of the social covenant (social injustice), and in a devastation of the covenant with nature (drought, pollution, blight—

see, for example, Isa. 24). A restoration of fidelity to God brings a restoration of the conditions of social justice in human relations and of benign relations between society and nature. The social and the natural languages are so intimately integrated that it is something of a distortion even to speak of them as two different relations, rather than as parts of a single socionatural covenant that binds the creation into one community. Humanity, not nature, is the contrary element from whence arises disobedience. Old Testament religion concentrates on restoring humanity to the sovereignty of God, as the discordant element that breaks the community of creation.

Unlike the Greek and Christian traditions, the Old Testament is patriarchal without linking this to an alienated view of creation. Indeed the hostile actions of the natural environment are often identified with the activity of God in punishing Israel for "her" wayward (harlot) activity. The language of God toward Israel is modeled on patriarchal domination of males over females, fathers over children. But the natural world remains an autonomous sphere of God's dominion and the revelation of divine power and glory that God can use for or against Israel. Only in the context of Israel's fidelity to God does nature become benign toward the human community. It is not a neutral sphere upon which ruling males can impose their own desires.

Two important elements which unite class and sexist languages to a view of nature as a sphere of human domination and repression are absent from the psalms and the prophets. One element is that view which regards consciousness as transcendent to visible nature, while the bodily sphere is seen as ontologically and morally inferior, to be subjugated by the superior principle represented by the mind. The second element absent from the Old Testament is the reading of the spirit-nature split into class and sexist relations, so that women, slaves, and lower classes are seen as analogous to the inferior realm of bodily "nature," while ruling-class males identify themselves with transcendent spirit.

These two elements, absent from pre-exilic Old Testament religion, are typical of classical philosophy. Here the authentic self is regarded as the soul or transcendent rationality, over against bodily existence. As we have seen, the relation of spirit to body is one of repression, subjugation, and mastery. Material existence is ontologically inferior to mind and the root of moral evil. Moreover, the language of hierarchical dualism is identified with social hierarchy. The hierarchy of spirit over body is expressed in the dominion of males over females, freedmen over slaves, Greeks over "Barbarians." Domination is "naturalized," so that the inferior ontological and moral characteristics of body in relation to mind are identified with the inferior psychobiological "natures" of women and subjugated classes.

After the fourth century B.C. the more optimistic ideal of Hellenic culture of harmony of body and spirit gave way to a pessimistic world alienation. Plato was the precursor of a quest for salvation viewed as flight from activity and material existence. Aristotle gave explicit form to the implicit misogynism of Plato's ontological hierarchicalism. Later Platonism fused elements from the two into an ascetic, misogynist world fleeing religious philosophy. This mood of world alienation—again, as detailed above—links with developments in Judaism in the Hellenistic period. In the apocalyptic writings (*ca.* 200 B.C. to A.D. 130), the "world" is seen as having slipped out of the sovereignty of God. Not God, but diabolic powers exercise immediate mastery over the world. The prophetic split between apostasy and future hope has become dualistic and otherworldly. Salvation now requires the destruction of the present created world and the creation of a new spiritual universe where Israel can be redeemed and God reign. Human hopes and the absolutism of God's demands have split apart what earlier biblical faith had held together in dialectical unity. Transcendent hope and commandment demand an infinite and immortal world that shatters the limits of the original created order of God. Gnostic radicals did not hesitate to suggest that the creator of the present world, the God of the Old Testament, was not the true God, but a demon.

Christianity was born through a fusion of apocalyptic Judaism and Platonic dualism. Despite the efforts of the Church Fathers to knit back together the God of creation and the God of eschatological redemption, cosmic alienation and spiritual dualism triumphed in classical Christian spirituality. But the Christian theological synthesis, which reigned from the patristic era through seventeenth-century Protestant orthodoxy, was hardly a theology that secularized the world as a sphere of neutral human domination. The Christian view of nature split creation into two opposite possibilities: sacramentality and demonization. Nature, restored to the sovereignty of God through Christ, was exemplified in the sacraments. Here, in the sacral sphere conquered by the Church, nature once more shone forth as the image and incarnate presence of God. But, outside this sphere of redemption, nature was demonic and alien to God, an outer darkness where Satan and his evil host abounded. A secular science that would seek to free itself from ecclesiastical control would be regarded as falling into this demonic sphere and tantamount to the Faustian alliance with the devil. For classical Christianity, nature could be sacramental or demonic, but never secular, i.e., never neutral and "value-free." Classical Protestantism, just as vehemently as Catholicism, would see "fallen" nature as demonic, while assaulting and shrinking the sense of nature as sacramental.[4] Again, it is not accidental that renewed demonology and witch hunts abounded in the era of religious warfare between Catholics and Protestants, and both saw their stereotypic victim as an evil, lusty female.

In order to render the world benign and available for human use, nature, demonized by Christianity, had to be exorcised. The Renaissance humanists failed to accomplish this because, although they affirmed that the spirit of nature was indeed benign and serviceable to human commandments, their method was one that reinterpreted magic as white rather than black. Science for them was still in the framework of a magical world-view that manipulated nature through its psychospiritual affinities with the human soul.[5] Francis Bacon recognized the need to break this tie of science to a magical world-view. He sought to bring the project of scientific domination of nature under the aegis of Christian respectability by declaring that the domination of nature through science was actually the fulfillment of the ancient Christian hope for the redemption of nature. But covertly he also created a quite unchristian split between the moral redemption of the human soul and the restoration of nature. The former was the sphere of religion and the latter was the sphere of science. But the two had become disconnected, so that nature restored to the domination of "reason" fell under "man" (ruling males) as God's agent. Subjugation of nature to human reason could be equated with restoration of creation to divine sovereignty, without questioning the moral nature of "man." The split between science and morality, between the external project of domination and the internal project of human regeneration, neutralized scientific technology and allowed all extension of power over nature to be regarded as value-free and morally unquestionable.[6]

Liberalism was the social philosophy that flowed out of the optimistic hopes of scientific rationalism for continual improvement of society through science. Liberalism was based on two overt premises: the secularization of nature and the universalism of the category "man." Nature was stripped of a potential for sacrality (or demonization). It became objectified as a sphere conforming solely to the rules of mathematical reason. Descartes divorced totally the opposite "natures" of thought and extension, yet the latter conformed to the former as object of knowledge to instrumental knower. No internal moral doubts or external demonic fears need inhibit its full exploitation for the ends desired by "man" (ruling males). The world had been thoroughly "thingified" as an object for use.[7]

But liberalism also broke down the naturalized orders of traditional hierarchical society that divided people into priests, lords, and serfs: head-people and body-people. An abstract equalitarianism, based on the possession by all "men" of practical rationality, united the human essence in a single definition. Theoretically, now, neither class division, race division, nor sex division could be justified on the grounds of differences of "nature," representing the split between spirit and body. All social revolutionary movements that seek to overthrow the rule of the feudal and then the bourgeois classes, white domination and male domination, draw on this tradition of democratic, universal human "nature."

Yet liberalism remained limited in its willingness to actualize this equalitarianism. It could espouse a generalized civil rights for "all," but this was exercised in practice by free, propertied males. It did not envision the restructuring of economic relations that would make equality meaningful for the poor. Only a few daring liberals, such as Condorçet and John Stuart Mill, dared respond to the woman's movement by envisioning the inclusion of women in the "rights of man."[8] Yet even they insisted that woman's socioeconomic position would remain unchanged by this. Thus all but "exceptional women" would remain unable to exercise these expanded rights in practice. The category "man," in the ideology of "man's domination of nature," remained, therefore, a mystified code-language for male ruling-class domination of others through expanded productivity. The fruits of domination belonged to the dominant class, sex, and cultural group, structuring the new power gained from technology into a magnified war of oppression against dominated social groups. The crisis of ecology and technology reflects this context of social injustice and unequal power relations within which the industrial revolution arose and which it escalated into a global war of the rich against the poor for the resources of the earth.

The rise of secular industrialized society and the dissolution of the hierarchical society of feudal Christendom created a backlash in the form of reactionary, romantic, and racist movements. Liberalism purported to be based on a unitary essence of humanness, modeled on pragmatic rationality. Romanticism, by contrast, reflected the growing alienation of sensitive spirits to the dehumanization of the technological order, but also the fear of breakdown of organic, hierarchical society. Romanticism stressed the differences of "natures" according to race, class, and sex. Contrary types of human "essences," based on presumed hierarchies of being, again reappeared, rationalizing racist and sexist doctrines of inherent differences between Germans and Jews, Negroes and whites, males and females. Women again were said to be "closer to nature," less rational, inherently dependent, auxiliary rather than autonomous. A male alienation from technology and search for "reconciliation with nature" re-emphasized the identification of women with that nonrational "nature" which is the contrary of scientific technology. But the romantic flight from technology to "nature" only mystified the power relations between males and those groups that they identified with "nature," since the actual relation between the two continued to be one of domination augmented by monopoly of the fruits of technology. The romantic exploration of alienation remained aesthetic. It did not grapple with a socioeconomic or structural dissolution of domination.

Women seeking emancipation were caught on the horns of a false dilemma between reason and nature created by male culture. Women, ever the symbol of the sphere to be dominated, and hence also the symbol of the sphere from which males are alienated, were given the options of emancipation through identification with a misogynist male rationality or reidentification with a concept of "nature" and "femininity" which ever returns them to powerless, inarticulate subjugation.[9]

The nineteenth-century concept of "progress" materialized the Judeo-Christian God concept. Males, identifying their egos with transcendent "spirit," made technology the project of progressive incarnation of transcendent "spirit" into "nature." The eschatological god became a historical project. Now one attempted to realize infinite demand through infinite material "progress," impelling nature forward to infinite expansion of productive power. Infinite demand incarnate in finite nature, in the form of infinite exploitation of the earth's resources for production, results in ecological disaster: the rapid eating up of the organic foundations of life under our feet in an effort to satisfy ever-growing appetites for goods. The matrix of being, which is no less the foundation of human being, is rapidly depleted. Within two centuries this pattern of thought and activity has brought humanity close to the brink of the destruction of the earth and its environment.

It is not too extreme to see this denouement as inherent in the fundamental patriarchal revolution of consciousness that sought to deny that the spiritual component of humanity was a dimension of the maternal matrix of being. Patriarchy sought to elevate consciousness to supernatural apriority. Mother and nature religion traditionally have seen heaven and earth, gods and humans, as dialectical components within the primal matrix of being. Its spirituality was built on the cyclical ecology of nature, of death and rebirth. Patriarchal religion split

apart the dialectical unities of mother religion into absolute dualism, elevating a male-identified consciousness
to transcendent apriority. Fundamentally this is rooted in
an effort to deny one's own mortality, to identify essential
(male) humanity with a transcendent divine sphere
beyond the matrix of coming-to-be-and-passing-away.
By the same token, woman became identified with the
sphere of finitude that one must deny in order to negate
one's own origins and inclusion in this realm. The
woman, the body, and the world were the lower half of a
dualism that must be declared posterior to, created by,
subject to, and ultimately alien to the nature of (male)
consciousness, in whose image man made his God.

Despite certain efforts to integrate the God of history
and the God of creation in the prophets, apocalyptic religion moves toward the annihilation of nature by a God of
transcendent history. The existing world is perceived as
inadequate to the demands of this transcendent God. It
must finally be destroyed in order to make a "new creation" which does not rest on spaciotemporal limits, but
comes down from "heaven." Patriarchal religion ends
not only in judgment upon the intractability of human
moral turpitude (identified with the female realm of "carnality"), but with a perception of the finite cosmos itself
as evil in its intractability to reformation by infinite demand. It must be destroyed so it can be replaced by an
infinite eternal world made in the image of infinite consciousness. The patriarchal self-deception about the origins of consciousness ends logically in the destruction
of the earth.

It is characteristic of the male ideology of transcendent
dualism that it cannot enter into reciprocity with the
"other." Its view of what is over against itself is not that
of the conversation of two subjects, but of the conquest
of an alien object. The intractability of the other side of
the dualism to its demands does not suggest that the
"other" has a "nature" of her own that needs to be re-

spected and with which one must enter into conversation. Rather, this intractability is seen as that of disobedient rebellion. For Plato, the resistance of the primal matrix to formation by infinite ideals is regarded as the intrinsically evil character of "matter," which indicates its inferior moral and ontological nature. Women are the primary symbols of this lower moral and ontological sphere which is to be repressed and subjugated. In social terms this means that women are cut out of the "progress" of male civilization. They are forbidden to participate in the formation of its sanctioning religious, educational, and political processes. While males use knowledge to free themselves from biological determination, women are subjugated all the more to exclusively biological porcesses. They are forbidden knowledge and control of the technology that would place their own biological processes in their own hands (contraception, abortion, gynecology). Thus the structures of patriarchal consciousness that destroy the harmony of nature are expressed symbolically and socially in the repression of women.

INDUSTRIAL SOCIETY AND THE SUBJUGATION OF WOMEN

Sexism and ecological destructiveness are related in the symbolic patterns of patriarchal consciousness, but they also take intensive socioeconomic form in modern industrial society. Rapid industrialization went hand in hand with the depletion of the economic functions of women traditionally centered around the home. Industrialization also drew many poor women into the factory at exploitative wages, far below those even of the exploited male worker. But industrial society transformed the relationship of the home to economic production. The very word *economy* originally meant "functions of the home." Originally, except for a few luxury items, the basic economic

processes of daily life, both of food growing and processing and of manufacture of tools and goods, went on
in or contiguous with the home. Industrialization meant
the progressive alienation of more and more productive
processes from the home. Male work, once taking place
in farms and shops in or around the home, became increasingly disconnected with the home and collectivized
in a separate sphere. Women more and more lost their
own productive work, as well as their integration with
male work. The home was refashioned from a producer
to a consumer unit in society, totally dependent upon a
separate work structure no longer under its control. The
work of the home and hence of women became concentrated on intensive interpersonal emotionality, extended
child nurture, and the primary physical support (eating,
sleeping) of male work. A new type of family and a new
definition of woman's "place" that had never existed before in so narrow a form came into being for the bourgeois woman. Having lost the productive functions that
had been theirs in preindustrial society, they were
confined exclusively to the spheres of reproduction, intensive child-rearing, emotional compensation, and the
housekeeping functions (with the loss of servants) that
free the bourgeois male for the industrial workday.

The confining of women to a home defined as the
sphere of "love," child nurture, and housekeeping
forced them into a new underdevelopment, in contrast to
the nineteenth-century feminist quest for increased education and activity (indeed, becoming the contradiction
that helped create this feminist demand). Women's careers became children. Population began to expand rapidly in the industrial era until it reached today's crisis proportions. Today an ecologically sound population policy
would demand that most couples have two children and
some have less, in order to reduce the population to
safer levels. Yet the social ideology of woman's role continues to insist that women build their entire lives and

identities (with an increasing life expectancy) around the nurture of less and less children. It is hardly surprising that modern women are afflicted by a desperate vacuity.

Victorian society attempted to pacify the contradiction between the growing woman's consciousness and the depleted functions of woman's "sphere" by the idealization of domesticity. But this was developed under the traditional Christian psychology of sexual repression. By the turn of the century the contradiction between intensified domesticity and sexual repression became so violent that the underside of Victorian society exploded in the Freudian revolution. But Freudianism, as we have seen, was unwilling to criticize the socioeconomic basis of female "hysteria," and so its lifting of the skirts of sexual repression was fed back into a renewed intensification of female suppression. A greater recognition of sexuality was integrated into the psychology of the bourgeois family as an integral element of its maintenance. The eroticization of the private sector of life is deliberately stimulated in capitalist society to compensate for and pacify male alienation from, and loss of control over, the work and political processes and to intensify the compensatory role of women and the home. Women are trapped in the private sector to service these male compensatory needs. They become not only the full-time child nurturers, but also the ideal friend and the sexual playmate, creating for themselves an illusory sense of a multiplicity of important roles.[10]

The eroticization of private life around the home also stimulates its function as the prime consumer unit in an economic system built on increasing consumption of products, most of which glut the appetites but distort basic needs. Through advertising, the imagination of society is invaded by artificial needs for products designed to decay and be replaced rapidly. Women become both the chief buyer and the sexual image through which the appetites of consumption are stimulated. Woman becomes a self-alienated "beautiful object" who sells her own quickly decaying façade to herself. Deprived of an integral existence, she exists to be seen and used by others, like eye makeup, which does not help a woman to see, but turns her eyes into objects to be seen. She is both the image and the manager of a home which is to be converted into a voracious mouth, stimulated by the sensual image of the female, to devour the products of consumer society. A continual stream of garbage flows forth in increasing quantity from this home, destroying the earth. Yet the home and women are not the originator but the victim of this system.[11]

As we have seen in earlier discussions, the split between the consumer home and alienated work was sanctified in Protestant theology, the theology of bourgeois society, in the form of the split between "moral man and immoral society." Reinhold Niebuhr became the chief formulator of this essential dichotomy in bourgeois culture between the home and public life.[12] With the secularization of society, religion and morality become feminized or privatized. Morality becomes appropriate only to the individual person-to-person relation exemplified by marriage. Love morality is "unrealistic" in the public sphere. Here the only possible morality is that of a "justice" defined as a balancing of competitive egoism. Women become pre-eminently the symbol of the private sphere of altruistic "morality." They are pre-eminently "moral man," while the male sphere of public life becomes rational in a way that is emptied of human values. Morality is privatized, sentimentalized, and identified with the "feminine" in a way that both conceals the essential immorality of sexism and rationalizes a value-free public world. A morality defined as "feminine" has no place in the "real world" of competitive male egoism and technological rationality.

The domestication of morality and religion in bourgeois culture also becomes a new "law" by which women are morally forbidden to "leave the home" and participate in the public world of men. It is now argued that this implies no inferiority in the view of women, but rather, a recognition of her "superior moral nature" which exists by virtue of her identification with the moral sphere of the "home." To step out of this sanctuary to enter the "dirty world" of business and politics would only lower woman's "nature" and prevent her from "elevating the world" through that "uplifting" influence that she exercises from the "home." [13] All this language, of course, totally mystifies the powerless, dependent status of women and the relation of the home to society. The emptying of the public realm of the humanistic values represented by personal morality also makes careers in politics, business, and technology uncongenial to the kinds of personalities developed in women. Women's education is concentrated on the "humanities," and women are generally undereducated in scientific and technological knowledge. This reinforces their psychological aversion to the most critical areas where real power is exercised in society and their decision to confine themselves to the home or to seek careers only in those auxiliary spheres, such as nursing and social work, that extend the work of the home, but without challenging the antihuman values of the public realm.

Women should look with considerable suspicion upon the ecological band-aids presently being peddled by business and government to overcome the crisis of exploitative technology. The ideology which splits private morality from public business will try to put the burden of ecological morality on the private sector. To compensate for the follies of the system, the individual consumers will be asked to tighten their belts; the system itself will not be challenged to change. Changes in the consumption patterns of the home can only be tokenism, since ecological immorality belongs to the patterns of production and social exploitation that is systemic. The home is its victim and tool, but not the originator of these patterns. A society which makes the individual worker totally dependent on the private auto for transportation is not serious when it asks that private worker to change his or her patterns of gas consumption, since there is no alternative method by which the home can be linked to the worlds of work and shopping necessary for survival. The auto is not a private luxury, but a systemic element that links all the other elements of the system to the home. Reforms directed at the private sphere can only be tokenism. Women will naturally be pressed into becoming the self-help ecologists in band-aid remedies that increase the dissipation of their energies in trivia, but have minimal effects on the ecological imbalances.

Ecological morality aimed at the home must also turn ecological concern itself into a new consumer product for women's use. The ecological factor will be built into consumer products in some trivial way and then sold with much advertising to women as a luxury item tacked onto present consumer products to placate the conscience.

The actual patterns of rapid destruction of the raw materials necessary to maintain the existing level of industrial production is already creating a world crisis and will soon result in economic devolution and declining production worldwide, only temporarily staved off by intensified search for untapped raw materials and energy resources. Women are on the bottom of those groups who are "last hired and first fired." Women have been forced into production in large numbers only when war production artificially escalates the need for industrial workers, while draining off the males available for such work. Thus in any situation of declining production, working-class women will be the first to be laid off in industry and women in all professions marginalized in a shrinking job market. The demand of women for more jobs thus must inevitably meet with new strategies of domestication by male-dominated society. A failing affluence and productivity, structured on the present distribution of power, means that the present elites (male, white, upper class) will try to be the last to lose their affluence and high-consumption patterns. Upper-class Western white males will try to shift the burdens of a declining job market to those who are marginal and dependent, the groups who are regarded as surplus labor or sources for raw materials (women, the jobless poor, the third world). Thus the claim of a capitalist-oriented "development" to gradually overcome the present patterns of social injustice, through expansion of its present system of production, must be regarded as increasingly fallacious.

This does not mean that the resources of the earth were not originally and are perhaps not still now capable of supporting a postscarcity, ecologically balanced society, where everyone is given meaningful social activity. It simply means that this cannot happen by infinite expansion of the present patterns based on unjust social relations between the sexes, classes, and nations and a destructive relation to the earth. All dependent or impoverished groups must look to the disappointment of their hopes for inclusion in Western affluence through the expansion of this model of development. The Western pattern of industrialization cannot include traditionally dependent groups because it is based on the rape of the raw materials of the globe to feed an affluent elite. To expand this level of production worldwide for all would destroy the raw materials and poison the ecological systems of the entire world in a few decades. The earth cannot long support the maintenance of this style of industrialization, much less expand it in depth to the poor. What appears to be an internationalization of this system at present reflects only the neocolonialism of domination of world resources by an international cartel, not the spread of affluence downward to the masses.

Women too must recognize the fallacy of the claim to include them as active contributors in the present economic system by its infinite expansion. Only in the heroic age of rapid industrialization in the West, and in a similar period of rapid industrial revolution in communist countries, have women been invited to participate in industrial work in large numbers, although, even in Marxist countries, seldom on equal terms with male workers. Wartime also becomes a time when even fascist countries put aside their sexism to invite "Rosie the Riveter" to come into the factory to maintain the industry of the Fatherland, while the males hurl the fruits of her womb and her hands at each other. In wartime, too, women are encouraged to attend universities in greater numbers, to fill the places of absent males. This has no connection with translating their education into jobs, however, which must be reserved for returning males. Expanded job opportunities for women have happened when there is a great need for "hands" because of these kinds of special crises. But the overall pattern of industrial society has been one which marginalized women's participation in the economy and must be expected to do so more as this system begins to fail.

Finally women must look with suspicion on the symbolic role they will be asked to play in an ecological crisis analyzed within patriarchal culture. Any effort to reconcile such a male with "nature," which does not restructure the psychology and social patterns which make nature "alien," will tend to shape women, the patriarchal symbol of "nature," into romanticized servitude to a male-defined alienation. The concern with ecology could repeat the mistakes of nineteenth-century romanticism with its renewed emphasis on the opposite, "complementary natures" of men and women. Women will again be asked to be the "natural" wood-nymph and earth mother and to create places of escape from the destructive patterns of the dominant culture. Women will be told that their "highest calling" is to service this type of male need for sex, rest, emotionality, and escape from reality in a simulated grassy flower Eden. But the real power structures that are creating the crisis will be unaffected by such leisure-time games. Many women in the fundamentalist and communal movements have already been suckered into these roles based on romantic male escapism.[14] Women must recognize that they represent the oldest and ultimate ideology of patriarchal culture, who serve to maintain its patterns of male domination and world exploitation. Already aspects of the ecological, communal, ahd human potential movements are deeply infected by this type of romantic escapism which evades the real structure of the problem while recreating women's role as the symbol and servant of male self-alienation.

WOMEN'S LIBERATION, ECOLOGY, AND SOCIAL REVOLUTION

Women must see that there can be no liberation for them and no solution to the ecological crisis within a society whose fundamental model of relationships continues to be one of domination. They must unite the demands of the women's movement with those of the ecological movement to envision a radical reshaping of the basic socioeconomic relations and the underlying values of this society. The concept of domination of nature has been based from the first on social domination between master and servant groups, starting with the basic relation between men and women. An ecological revolution must overthrow all the social structures of domination. This means transforming that world-view which underlies domination and replacing it with an alternative value system. It is here that the values and development learned in the patriarchal family and in the local community are of great importance. How do we change the self-concept of a society from the drives toward possession, conquest, and accumulation to the values of reciprocity and acceptance of mutual limitation? It is hard even to imagine a coherent alternative beyond the present horizons of crisis and impending disaster. Even when reasonable and possible alternatives can be sketched, the practical power to counteract the systems which perpetuate the world of global exploitation and war escape us. We seem to be awaiting a planetary rebirth which can come about only when massive catastrophe decisively discredits the present systems of power. We scarcely know whether either the physical or the spiritual resources exist to make such a creative leap beyond disaster. So it is with fear and trembling that we even try to dream of new things.[15]

First of all, harmony between the human community and natural systems has nothing to do with anti-intellectual or antitechnological primitivism. The human capacity for technological rationality is itself the highest gift of nature. It needs to be freed from its captivity to ruling-class domination and not be regarded as inherently evil. Escapist, romantic primitivism tends to be the response of alienated children of the elite. It has little to offer those left out of the present affluence. What is needed is democratization of decision-making over technological development and equalization of its benefits. It must become impossible for a small ruling class to monopolize the wealth from world resources, while transferring the social costs to the people in the form of poisoned air, water, and soil. This also demands the development of new ecological technology oriented toward preservation of the earth.

Some obvious changes are necessary. High on the agenda is a total overhaul of the present method of transportation that is based on the private auto and the freeway system. The gasoline auto will have to be phased out, to be replaced by public mass transit between urban centers, and bicycles and electric cars and buses within local areas. Congested areas should be cleared of trucks or cars entirely, to allow only bicycles or pedestrians. We are fully capable of designing such an alternative, but lack of coordinated planning and commitment of politicians to the present automobile, trucking, and oil interests keeps us tied to a transportation system that is heading for disaster. There must be a general shift from energy sources which are polluting and limited to those which are nonpolluting and renewable, such as sun, wind, water, electricity, and perhaps nuclear energy, if ways can be found to handle its wastes. Clearly an ecological technology will demand great scientific imagination, but an imagination directed toward the common good of the entire world community and one which seeks to integrate the human sociosphere into the biosphere of nature in a positively reinforcing relationship.

It seems possible that, as disasters mount from the present unregulated system, there may come a time when the major systems of power in the United States, Russia, and perhaps even China would move together to create a global planned society. This will be called a "socialist revolution," and many well-meaning liberals will be convinced that democracy must be sacrificed for human survival. Even persons such as Henry Kissinger have been free to suggest that democracy's days are numbered.[16] One can well imagine a sudden unanimity about this among right-wing and left-wing world leaders, all of whom are basically fascists. Some unified management of world resources is needed, so that national rivalries cease to keep the planet in a permanent state of economic and military warfare. The destruction of our resources in war technology and its threat to survival must be ended. But if that government is to be other than totalitarian, managed for the benefit of a world ruling class, socialist communities must be built from the bottom up.[17]

A democratic socialism has to be a communitarian socialism. This means the economic and political sectors of local communities are run on the principles of subsidiarity, self-ownership, and self-management. Planning, distribution, and enforcement of standards need to be ceded to larger units: metropopitan regions, states, nations, and international bodies. But these levels of government must be rooted in strong self-governing local communities, with representatives elected from the base. Only in this way can socialism be kept from becoming total alienation of the atomized individual in huge impersonal corporatisms. An urgent task for those concerned about the society of the future is the development of viable forms of local communalization on the level of residential groups, work places, and townships that can increase our control over the quality of our own lives.

It is on the level of the local community that socialism can change the dependency of women by transforming the relationship among power, work, and home. The nuclear family cannot overcome the caste status of women because it is the victim of a rigid complementarity of work-home, male-female dualities. As we saw earlier, Marxist or state socialism has tended to solve this by giving over female work to state agencies in order to integrate women into productive labor. The strategy of a communitarian socialist society is different. It would bring work back into an integrated relationship to self-governing living communities. Women's work is still communalized and professionalized, but control over these functions remains with families themselves who band together in groups on the level appropriate for particular functions. For example, a residential group would develop communal shopping, cooking, child care, cleaning, or gardening by collectivizing its own resources. The child is not taken out of the family into an impersonal state agency to free the mother for other activity. Rather, it gains a tribe while remaining rooted in the family.

Communalization of functions of local groups should

not be confused with what is called a commune in contemporary America, i.e., eight or ten young adults in a house built for a nuclear family. This is an unstable unit at best. What we are talking about is the principle of the kibbutz, but applied in a diversity of forms to different living and working patterns. Communalized living requires a new architecture which balances private and corporate dimensions of life. It calls for new urban planning to integrate living with work. Clear, objective political forms that maximize personal participation need to be developed. Short-term committees with rotating membership who bring propositions before a direct primary assembly would be my own preference. Models for such communities are not beyond our reach. We have a long tradition of Christian communitarianism to draw from. Even residential colleges, although not fully democratic, are a well-accepted example of a self-governing community for work and living.

I will outline a few of the ways in which socialized local communities could greatly alter the traditional role of women. Communalization of child-raising in residential groups or even in work places could change the child-bearing patterns in nuclear families. The isolated family tries to have several children in order to create a mini-community. In a communal family, children would grow up with a sense of a large group of "brothers and sisters." A bonding of children of a group of families would develop, extending the child's own peer group and also gaining relations with a large group of other adults who are personally concerned with her or him. The personal child-parent relationship would not be destroyed, but it would be supplemented by a larger group of siblings, mothers and fathers, and older brothers and sisters, much as is the case today where the family is still rooted in clan and tribe. Adults who do not have their own children would also have an opportunity to nurture and develop the lives of children. Children would have a sense of a variety of other adults, older children and peers to whom they could turn for resources that might not exist in their immediate families. Fifty adults might have between them about twenty or twenty-five children, which would still afford a bountiful community of children, but rapidly return the population to a level which the earth would be better able to support.

The tasks of housekeeping, child-raising, food procurement and preparation would be communalized and spread between men and women. One sexual group would no longer be structured into exclusive responsibility for this type of work, isolated from each other and from the work places. Those who chose to be managers of these functions would be skilled professionals and suitably rewarded. Dimensions of private life and control over personal needs would still be retained, allowing for individual choice in relating private and communal aspects of life. The communalization of much of the equipment of daily life—such as communal kitchens, communally owned vehicles and tools signed out on need—could drastically reduce the present patterns of consumption, waste, and duplication of equipment in nuclear families. A decentralized economy would return much of the production to small factories, workshops, and farms owned and run by the local community. Materials would be made to be long-lasting. The shoddy goods made to decay and be replaced rapidly in the profit economy would lose their rationale. There would also return a pride in craftsmanship essential to the de-alienation of labor. Home and work, production and consumption, field and factory would be related organically, making each human group aware of the ecological relations of its own material life with that of nature. Human society, patterned for a balance through diversity, would be consciously integrated into its environment. The key to this integration is the use of wastes. In an ecologically balanced society, there should be no real "waste." In effect, the wastes of each system should become converted into being the fuel or food of another system in a recycling process that continually renews and beautifies the environment.

Since local communities would make many of the decisions that affect their immediate lives, self-government would counteract much of the present sense of alienation and powerlessness of the atomized individual. The interrelationship of home and work would allow men and women to take an equal hand in both nurturing and supportive roles and also in work and political life. The split between alienated work life and shrunken domesticity, which segregates women on one side of this divide, would be overcome by bridging the gap between the two, rather than by abolishing and devaluing the roles of family life. Not only would women be allowed the participation in the larger social processes that they have historically been denied, but men also would recover the affective and nurturing roles with children and other people historically denied them, which has repressed the gentle, humane side of males and shaped the male personality into that hyper-aggressivity and antagonistic combativeness that has been called "masculine." Without sex-role stereotyping, sex-personality stereotyping would disappear, allowing for genuine individuation of personality. Instead of being forced into a mold of masculine or feminine "types," each individual could shape a complex whole from the full range of human psychic potential for intellect and feeling, activity and receptivity. A richer pattern of friendship could also develop among adults, diffusing the often over-exclusivism of the nuclear marriage that makes two married adults each other's sole personal nurturers of personal intimacy over a lifetime.

The center of such a new society would have to be not just the appropriate new social form, but a new social vision, a new soul that would inspire the whole. Society

would have to be transfigured by the glimpse of a new
type of social personality, a "new humanity" appropriate
to a "new earth." One might call this even a "new religion," if one understands by this the prophetic vision to
shape a new world on earth, and not an alienated spirituality.[18] A society no longer bent on "conquering the
earth" might, however, also have more time for the cultivation of interiority, for contemplation, for artistic work
that celebrated being for its own sake. But such interiority would not be cultivated at the expense of the community, as in monastic escape from "the world." It would be
a cultivation of the self that would be at one with an
affirmation of others, both our immediate neighbors and
all humanity and the earth itself, as that "thou" with
whom "I" am in a state of reciprocal interdependence.

Such solidarity is not utopian, but eminently practical,
pointing to our actual solidarity with all others and with
our mother, the earth, which is the actual ground of our
being. Perhaps this also demands a letting-go of that
self-infinitizing view of the self that culminates in the wish
for personal immortality. One accepts the fact that it is
the whole, not the individual, which is that "infinite" out
of whose womb we arise at birth and into whose womb
we are content to return at death, using the human capacity for consciousness, not to alienate ourselves from
nature, but rather, to nurture, perfect, and renew her natural harmonies, so that earth might be fair, not only for us
and our children, but for all generations of living things
still to come.

Notes

1. William Leiss, *The Domination of Nature* (New York: Braziller, 1972), p. 55, n. 14.

2. Lynn White, "The Religious Roots of Our Ecological Crisis," *Science*, 155 (1967): 1203–7. Theodore Roszak's *Where the Wasteland Ends* (Garden City, N.Y.: Doubleday, 1973) is, among other things, a strong statement of the bankruptcy of the Christian tradition as regards the crisis of technology and the need to return to nature religion. The Indian theologian, Vine Deloria, in *God Is Red* (New York: Grosset and Dunlap, 1973), repudiates Christianity, but finds affinities between the Indian ecological perspective and the religion of the Old Testament.

3. H. H. Hvidberg, *Weeping and Laughter in the Old Testament* (Leiden: Brill, 1962).

4. Richard Slotkin, *Regeneration through Violence* (Middletown, Conn.: Wesleyan University Press, 1973), shows the relationship between the theological view of nature as fallen and a demonic concept of the wilderness and the Indian in American Puritanism.

5. Frances Yates, *Giordiano Bruno and the Hermetic Tradition* (Chicago: University of Chicago Press, 1964).

6. Leiss, *op. cit.*, pp. 45–71.

7. Basil Willey, *Eighteenth Century Background: Studies on the Idea of Nature* (New York: Columbia University Press, 1941); also R. G. Collingwood, *The Idea of Nature* (London: Oxford University Press, 1960).

8. See above, chap. 1, n. 23.

9. Walter Houghton, *The Victorian Frame of Mind, 1830–1870* (New Haven: Yale University Press, 1957), chap. 13; also J.-J. Rousseau, *Emile: Or Education* (1762) (New York: Dutton, 1933), last chapter on the education of Sophie. For the extreme stereotypes of women in romanticism, see Mario Praz, *The Romantic Agony* (New York: Oxford University Press, 1951).

10. Barbara Welter, "The Cult of True Womanhood, 1820–1860," *American Quarterly*, 18 (Summer 1966); Dorothy

Bass Fraser, "The Feminine Mystique, 1890–1910," *Union Seminary Quarterly Review*, Summer 1972, pp. 225ff.; R. Ruether, "The Cult of True Womanhood," *Commonweal*, Nov. 9, 1973, pp. 127–32.

11. Betty Friedan, *The Feminine Mystique* (New York: Norton, 1963), was the catalytic statement of the relationship between the ideology of femininity and the woman's consumer role. H. Marcuse, *One Dimensional Man* (Boston: Beacon Press, 1964), pp. 71–78, has some pithy things to say about the use of the erotic image in modern consumer society.

12. Reinhold Niebuhr, *Moral Man and Immoral Society* (New York: Scribner's, 1932), pp. 257–58; also W. Rauschenbusch, *Christianity and Social Crisis* (New York: Macmillan, 1907), pp. 276–79.

13. See above, chap. 1, n. 27.

14. Traditionalism toward women in religious communal groups is evident in the Brüderhof; see Benjamin Zablocki, *The Joyful Community* (Baltimore, Md.: Penguin, 1972), pp. 117–22.

15. An effort to develop a strategy of change is found in George Lakey, *Strategy for a Living Revolution* (San Francisco: W. H. Freeman, 1973).

16. See Joseph Alsop, "Understanding Henry Kissinger," *The Washington Post*, Jan. 27, 1975 (editorial page, A section). An example of a liberal economist whose pessimistic forecasts for the future of humanity include the inevitable loss of democratic forms to totalitarian systems is Robert Heilbroner, *An Inquiry into the Human Prospect* (New York: Norton, 1974).

17. See Paul and Percival Goodman, *Communitas* (New York: Random House, 1947). also Murray Bookchin, *The Limits of the City* (New York: Harper & Row, 1973). Bookchin is presently working on a study of the relationship of ecology and communitarian socialism. His *The Ecology of Freedom* should be published by 1976.

18. Popular books on ecology and Christian reflection on ecology and theology, have multiplied in the late 1960s and the 1970s. But most Christian ecological theology has little realization of the relationship of social domination and ecological destruction and does not envision a new socioeconomic system. Typical examples of the literature are found

in Kenneth Alpers, "Starting Point for Ecological Theology;
A Bibliographical Survey," *New Theology, No. 8,* ed. Martin
Marty and Dean Peerman (New York: Macmillan, 1971), pp.
292ff. See also Ian Barbour, *Earth Might Be Fair* (Engle-
wood Cliffs, N.J.: Prentice-Hall, 1972), and J. B. Cobb, *Is It
Too Late? A Theology of Ecology* (New York: Bruce, 1971).

Select Bibliography:
Women's History

Bachofen, J. J. *Myth, Religion and Mother Right* (1861). Princeton: Princeton University Press, 1967.

Baer, Richard. *Philo's Use of the Categories of Male and Female*. Leiden: Brill, 1972.

Bailey, D. S. *The Man–Woman Relation in Christian Thought*. London: Longmans, 1959.

de Beauvoir, Simone. *The Second Sex*. New York: Bantam, 1953.

Bebel, August. *Women under Socialism*. New York: Schocken, 1971.

Blenkinsopp, Joseph. *Sexuality and the Christian Tradition*. Dayton, Ohio: Pflaum Press, 1969.

Cade, Tony. *The Black Woman*. New York: Signet, 1970.

von Campenhausen, Hans. *The Virgin Birth in the Theology of the Early Church*. Naperville, Ill.: Allenson, 1964.

Chavasse, Claude. *The Bride of Christ*. London: Faber and Faber, 1940.

Daly, Mary. *Beyond God the Father*. Boston: Beacon, 1973.

Daniélou, Jean. *The Ministry of Women in the Early Church*. London: Faith, 1961.

Diner, Helen. *Mothers and Amazons*. Garden City, N.Y.: Doubleday, 1973.

Ehrenreich, Barbara and Deirdre English. *Witches, Midwives and Nurses*. New York Feminist Press, 1973.

Engels, Friedrich. *The Origin and History of the Family, Private Property and the State* (1884). New York: International, 1963.

Farber, Thomas. *The Midwife and the Witch*. New Haven: Yale University Press, 1966.

Flexner, Eleanor. *Century of Struggle: The Women's Rights Movement in the United States.* New York: Atheneum, 1972.

Hays, H. R. *The Dangerous Sex: The Myth of Feminine Evil.* New York: Pocket Books, 1972.

Hernton, Calvin. *Sexism and Racism in America.* Garden City, N.Y.: Doubleday, 1965.

Hewitt, Emily C. and Suzanne R. Hiatt. *Women Priests: Yes or No?* New York: Seabury, 1973.

Heyer, Robert, ed. *Women and Orders.* New York: Paulist Press, 1974.

Horney, Karen. *Psychoanalysis and Women,* ed. J. B. Miller. Baltimore, Md.: Penguin, 1973.

Jewitt, Paul K. *Man as Male and Female.* Grand Rapids, Mich.: Eerdmans, 1975.

Kapelrud, A. S. *The Violent Goddess: Anath in the Ras Shamra Texts.* Oslo: Universitetsforlaget, 1969.

Kraditor, Aileen. *The Ideas of the Women's Suffrage Movement, 1890–1920.* Garden City, N.Y.: Doubleday, 1971.

Lenin, V. I. *The Emancipation of Women,* with appendix, "Lenin on the Woman Question," by Clara Zetkin. New York: International, 1972.

Lerner, Gerda. *Black Women in White America.* New York: Random House, 1972.

Miegge, Giovanni. *The Virgin Mary.* London: Lutterworth, 1955.

Mill, John Stuart. *The Subjugation of Women* (1869). Cambridge, Mass.: M.I.T. Press, 1970.

Miller, Jean Baker, ed. *Psychoanalysis and Women.* Baltimore, Md.: Penguin, 1973.

Mitchell, Juliet. *Psychoanalysis and Feminism.* New York: Pantheon, 1974.

Muncy, Raymond Lee. *Sex and Marriage in Utopian Communities: 19th Century America.* Baltimore, Md.: Penguin, 1974.

Neumann, Erich. *The Great Mother: An Analysis of the Archetype.* Princeton: Princeton University Press, 1963.

O'Meara, Thomas. *Mary in Protestant and Catholic Theology.* New York: Sheed and Ward, 1966.

O'Neill, William. *Everyone Was Brave: The Rise and Fall of Feminism in America.* Chicago: Quadrangle, 1969.

Patai, Raphael. *The Hebrew Goddess.* Philadelphia: Ktav, 1967.

Plumpe, Joseph. *Mater Ecclesia: An Inquiry into the Concept of the Church as Mother in Early Christianity.* Washington, D.C.: Catholic University of America Press, 1947.

Praz, Mario. *The Romantic Agony.* New York: Oxford, 1951.

Reik, Theodore. *The Creation of Woman.* New York: McGraw-Hill, 1960.

Robb, Theodore K. and Robert L. Rotberg, eds. *The Family in History.* New York: Harper & Row, 1971.

Rogers, Katherine. *The Troublesome Helpmate: A History of Misogyny in Literature.* Seattle: University of Washington Press, 1966.

Roszak, B. and T. *Masculine/Feminine.* New York: Harper & Row, 1969.

Rowbotham, Sheila. *Women, Resistance and Revolution.* New York: Random House, 1972.

Ruether, Rosemary and Eugene Bianchi, *From Machismo to Mutuality; Essays on Sexism.* New York: Paulist Press, 1975.

Ruether, Rosemary, ed. *Religion and Sexism: Images of Women in the Jewish and Christian Religious Traditions.* New York: Simon and Schuster, 1973.

Russell, Letty. *Human Liberation in a Feminist Perspective.* Philadelphia: Westminster, 1974.

Salper, Roberta. *Female Liberation: History and Current Politics.* New York: Knopf, 1972.

Scanzoni, L. and N. Hardesty, *All We're Meant to Be: A Biblical Approach to Women's Liberation.* Waco, Texas: Word Books, 1974.

Scott, Anne Firor. *The Southern Lady: From Pedestal to Politics, 1830–1930.* Chicago: University of Chicago Press, 1970.

Sherfey, Mary Jane. *The Nature and Evolution of Female Sexuality.* New York: Random House, 1972.

Slater, Philip. *The Glory of Hera: Greek Mythology and the Greek Family.* Boston: Beacon, 1968.

Staples, Robert. *The Black Family: Essays and Studies.* Belmont, Calif.: Wadsworth, 1971.

Stendahl, Krister. *The Bible and the Role of Women.* Philadelphia: Fortress, 1966.

Tavard, George. *Women in the Christian Tradition.* Notre Dame: Notre Dame University Press, 1973.

Welter, Barbara. "The Cult of True Womanhood, 1820–1860," *American Quarterly* 18 (Summer 1964), pp. 151–74.

Vicinus, Martha, ed. *Suffer and Be Still: Women in the Victorian Age.* Bloomington: Indiana University Press, 1973.

Index

Adler, Alfred, 142
Androgyny, 26, 57–8, 165
Anti-Semitism, 105–8
Aquinas, Thomas, 53, 72
Aristotle, 14–5, 189
Assumption (of Mary), 36, 50–1. *See also* Mariology

Bachofen, J. J., 5, 166–7
Bacon, Francis, 186, 191
Baltazar, Eulalio, 28
Black family, 117–20
Black movement, 132; and black church, 127; and black feminism, 129–31; and black nationalism, 128–9; male-oriented, 120, 126; and powerlessness of women, 126–7
Black Muslims, 128–9
Black theology, 115
Bulgakov, Sergius, 44–5

Castration-fear, 140–1, 144
Castration-trauma, 138–9, 141
Chesler, Phyllis, 150
Church, feminization of, 75–6
Cohn, Norman, 19
Communal family, 208–9
Communism, position of women in, 174–9

Communitarian socialism, 206–7
Comte, Auguste, 163, 166
Condorçet, A. N., 20, 192

Daly, Mary, 31, 36, 121
Davis, Elizabeth Gould, 5
deBeauvoir, Simone, 4
Deloria, Vine, 31
Deutsch, Helene, 142
Douglass, Frederick, 122

Earth-goddess, 12. *See also* Great Mother
Ecology, crisis of: alternative to, 204–8; and exploitation of women, 200–4; and industrialism, 193; religious roots of, 187; rooted in patriarchal consciousness, 194–6
Engels, Frederick, 3, 166–71, 173–4
Erikson, Erik, 138
Eschatological religion, 16, 109
Eve myth, interpretation of, 146–8

Female messiah, 164–5
Female, the (ideology of), 4–5; Christian symbols of, 42–5, 56; demonization

of, 18–9, 90–2; as inferior, 10–1, 13–5, 144; and sexual dualism, 17–23, 25–8, 74, 182
Fertility goddess. *See* earthgoddess; Great Mother
Feminism, 8, 121–3, 162, 179–80. *See also* Women's movement
Feminist theology, 115
Fourier, Charles, 163, 166
Freud, Sigmund, 137, 151–3; and female psychology, 138–41; post-Freudian criticism of, 142–5; feminist criticism of, 148–51

Goldmann, Emma, 171
Great Mother, 13, 40–1, 154–6

Hare, Nathan, 119
Holy Family, cult of, 20
Horney, Karen, 143
Housework, social critique of, 180–1

Immaculate conception, 53–5. *See also* Mariology
Industrialism, 166, 169, 196–200

Jesus (and women), 63–6
Jew, demonization of, 105–6
Jones, Mother, 171
Jung, C. G., 28, 36, 157–8; feminine principle in, 151–4

Leiss, William, 186
Lenin, V., 172–3
Liberalism, 191–3

Malleus Maleficarum, 19, 72, 97, 101
Marcuse, Herbert, 163
Mariology, 18–9, 36, 48–55; as liberating symbol, 56–8; in the New Testament, 46–7; prebiblical origins, 37
Marx, Karl, 166–7, 173
Mary (mother of Jesus). *See* Mariology
Mary Magdalene, 47, 49, 58, 64–5
Masters and Johnson, 145
Matriarchy, primitive, 5–6, 166–8
Menstruation, symbolism of, 15–6, 90
Mill, John Stuart, 192
Ministry: community-centered, 81–2; ordination of women to, 70–3, 78–80; of women in the New Testament, 63–9
Misogynism, 15, 20, 98, 143
Mitchell, Juliet, 150
Mother-goddess, 6, 11–3, 37–9, *See also* Great Mother
Murray, Margaret, 93

Nature, domination of, 13–4, 186; and patriarchal consciousness, 195–6; in prescientific thought, 187–91;

by reason and science, 191–4
Neumann, Erich, 154–8
Niebuhr, Reinhold, 199

Patai, Raphael, 41
Penis-envy, 139–40, 142–3, 151
Philips, McCandish, 108
Philo, 17
Plato, 189, 196
Proudhon, P. J., 162
Psychoanalysis, 137, 151, 158–9, 198. *See also* Freud, Sigmund; Jung, C. G.

Queen of Heaven, 39. *See also* Great Mother; Mother-goddess

Rank, Otto, 146
Reich, Wilhelm, 163
Reik, Theodore, 146–8
Rousseau, J. J., 162

St. Simonians, 162–3
Scroggs, Robin, 70
Shakers, 165
Sherfey, Mary Jane, 146
Socialism: Marxist, 166–73; utopian, 162–6

Tillich, Paul, 36
Transcendentalists, 165

Virginity, spiritual concept of, 17–9

White, Lynn, 187
Witches, 89–92, 97–99; belief in, 93–6, 100; and Jews, 105–7; persecution of, 18, 92, 100–5, 111 n. 1, 190
Women's movement, 3, 24–5, 29–31; and black liberation, 115–6, 121–3; class and race bias in, 124–5, 132; and sexual freedom, 163, 172–3; and socialism, 162–73